TRUE STORIES OF THE POWER OF THE ROSARY

The "Weapon that Wins All Battles"
With Scientific Evidence for the Faith

THOMAS CORBLEY

True Stories of the Power of the Rosary
The "Weapon that Wins All Battles" With Scientific Evidence for the Faith
Copyright © Thomas Corbley 2023

Published by Skinny Brown Dog Media
Atlanta | Punta del Este http://www.SkinnyBrownDogMedia.com

Distributed by Skinny Brown Dog Media
Design and composition by Skinny Brown Dog Media
Cover Design by Skinny Brown Dog Media

Library of Congress Cataloging-in-Publication Data Print
eBook ISBN: 978-1-957506-34-0
Hardback ISBN: 978-1-957506-35-7
Paperback ISBN: 978-1-957506-24-1
Case Laminate: 978-1-957506-35-7

WHAT YOUNG PEOPLE ARE SAYING ABOUT THIS BOOK

Anastasia (age 17): ... *I LOVE LOVE LOVE seeing this extra scientific evidence!!!!!!! ... Why isn't this taught on other theology books? This is the kind of information that me and my peers and seeking for, and no one seems to be able to give it. I love it!*

Nate (age 18): ... *I really liked the section on human blood on the shroud and how it converted the photographer. These sections included lots of information about the shroud I was not aware of and makes it pretty clear it is not a fake. ... I believe that reading this book has been helping me to pray more.*

Nick (age 24): *[Talking about Warriors For Mary group] I think this is great! It's a very good idea, and being in a group sounds excellent. I knew some people in the Catholic Campus Ministry that would've loved to have something like this.*

Yuliya (age 18): *I had very minimal prior knowledge and no particular interest in this subject, however the text did seem really interesting to me. I even recommended it to my mom after I was done reading and she found it really interesting as well ...*

DEDICATION:

I dedicate this book to the *Blessed Virgin Mary*, Queen of Heaven and Earth, Refuge of Sinners, Star of the Sea. She is an all powerful advocate with her Son, and she is the fastest way to reach Him. Were it not for her intercession, I wouldn't be here now. That, however, is a story for another day. May this book remain under Mary's patronage, and may she guide my mind and heart in pursuing this project to its completion.

I also dedicate the book to *Mom and Dad*. When I was fourteen, they inspired me to love the Rosary. They taught me how to pray it, and they prayed it with me.

There is no problem, I tell you, no matter how difficult it is, that we cannot solve by the prayer of the Holy Rosary. With the Holy Rosary we will save ourselves. We will sanctify ourselves. We will console Our Lord and obtain the salvation of many souls.

—Sister Lucia, visionary from the Church approved apparitions of Our Lady of Fatima

The soul which recommends itself to me by the recitation of the Rosary shall not perish.

—Blessed Virgin Mary to Saint Dominic

TABLE OF CONTENTS

INTRODUCTION: IT'S ALL ABOUT RELATIONSHIP

Behold, I stand at the door and knock.
If anyone hears my voice and opens the door,
[then] I will enter his house and dine with him,
and he with me. (Revelations 3:20)

How many people out there would be willing to be tortured to death for you? Tortured ... dragged through the streets ... surrounded by public laughter and ridicule? How many would be manhandled, mocked, blindfolded and then punched at will, followed by a brutal whipping, removing large portions of their skin and flesh, with thorns driven into their skull, finally dying upon an instrument of torture? How many would be willing to go through all of this ... for you?

How could anyone go through this? Why would anyone go through this? Why would someone suffer this extreme of human pain and misery?

RELATIONSHIP.

Anyone willing to sacrifice like this ... would have to be absolutely committed—perhaps desperately committed—to seeking a relationship with you.

This book introduces that Relationship. The same Person who suffered these things is seeking a relationship with you. As He says in the quote above, He wants to enter your house and dine with you. These are not the words of a distant God, floating around the universe. No, these are the words of a personal God.

What is this relationship like? How do I know that Jesus is Real ... that He isn't a fairly tale? What evidence ... scientifically analyzed physical evidence ... can I present that He is reaching out to you to establish this personal relationship?

Let me preview some of the evidence I'm referring to.

The Shroud of Turin, which many believe to be the burial cloth of Christ, shows the brutal torture of a man who suffered crucifixion. Some have concluded that this man received over six hundred wounds, including approximately one hundred and thirty scourges, nails driven through the hands and feet, and thorns driven into his head. Scientists have found real human blood on the Shroud, and by examining this blood, doctors have determined that this man suffered horrible, terrible pain, the kind of pain you would expect from a brutal torture. Scientists have also discovered an image on the linen cloth, an image of the face and body of a crucified man. This image is a photographic negative. Linen is not a photographic material, not even close. The Shroud of Turin is the most scientifically analyzed article in all of human history. It has been said that the ultraviolet light necessary to form the image on the Shroud exceeds the maximum power released by all ultraviolet light sources available for use today. To create this image on linen, it would require, among other things, pulses with intensities on the order of several billion watts. Could a dead body produce energy like this?

Some have claimed that a medieval counterfeiter forged the Shroud. Did the counterfeiter know about pollen tests, which didn't exist until centuries later? Pollen tests have found pollen on the Shroud from plants that grow in Jerusalem. Perhaps the counterfeiter also knew about limestone, found on the feet and knees of the man of the Shroud. The Shroud contains the rare Travertine Aragonite limestone, with its unique composition of strontium and iron, found in a specific tomb in Jerusalem. Travertine Aragonite limestone is found in Jerusalem and a few other places on earth. Did the counterfeiter know about photography, enabling him to create a perfect photographic negative image? Photography didn't exist until centuries later. Maybe the counterfeiter also knew about three-dimensional information, which he embedded into the image on the Shroud. How did the image get onto the Shroud?

Well known scientists have devised theories to account for the Shroud, with its many unusual characteristics. They have found evidence of particle and ultraviolet radiation emanating from the dead man's body. Dead bodies don't produce radiation. Could Jesus' Resurrection have produced radiation, leading to the unusual properties found on the Shroud of Turin? Could the Shroud provide evidence of Jesus' Resurrection? Is this the burial cloth of Christ?

Modern science has investigated Eucharistic Miracles where Hosts have turned into human heart tissue. The Church has recently approved miracles in Mexico, Poland and Argentina. Upon scientific analysis, the human heart tissue from these Hosts is found to be living. How is this possible? How can a Eucharistic Host turn into living heart tissue? These Eucharistic Miracles are extremely well documented and extensively analyzed by well known scientists. Scientists cannot explain them. Where did these tissue samples come from?

Juan Diego's tilma (or jacket) from the apparitions of Our Lady of Guadalupe has received almost endless scientific analysis. The tilma shows the image of a beautiful Lady, standing in front of the sun, her foot resting on a crescent moon, her hands joined in prayer and her head bowed in reverence. Juan Diego's tilma, made of plant fiber, should have lasted twenty or forty years, but it remains intact after four and a half centuries ... with unfaded colors. Numerous scientists have analyzed the tilma; they have conducted scientific studies on the colors, attempting to explain what type of color was used and how it was applied. They can't explain the image on the tilma. In fact, they can't even explain what the color is. Well-known scientists have studied the tilma extensively. Where did this image come from?

These three examples, the Shroud, Eucharistic Miracles and Juan Diego's tilma, are what I call the *"Big Three"*, three well-known examples of scientifically analyzed evidence for the faith. These examples have been diligently analyzed by well-known scientists, and science cannot explain them. They serve as physical evidence that Christianity is Real; Catholicism is Real and the faith is Real. I provide details on the Big Three next.

For the moment, however, I want to consider the immediate question. Why would Jesus produce miracles? Why would He provide scientifically analyzable evidence for our day and time, evidence that cannot be explained by the laws of modern science?

The answer is Relationship. He is reaching out to you, personally, to develop a relationship with you. He endured the misery of the cross because He was literally dying to have this relationship with you.

Why does Jesus want to develop a relationship with me? Why does Jesus want to share intimately in my life?

When you love someone, you want to be involved in their life, so Jesus is motivated by love. He thirsts for this relationship, and He died on the cross for each of us personally. His wounds testify to this love, and he suffered for your specific sins (as well for mine). However, there is a second reason. This reason is rarely talked about, but it shines forth in every page of the Bible. You're already very familiar with it; in fact, it's wired into your very being. God is calling you to go on a hero's journey[1], to fight against His enemies and save your generation.

What am I talking about? At this very moment, your generation, your brothers and sisters, are surrounded by enemies. Cyber-bullies are encouraging suicides; traffic fatalities are causing teen deaths; sex trafficking is destroying the lives of teens; incredibly pure opioids, like fentanyl, are causing drug overdoses, as cartels flood the U.S. market. School shootings and violence are rampant. In fact, less than five miles from my home a teen was recently stabbed to death in a McDonalds parking lot. Your generation is suffering from anxiety and depression. The twenty-first century is a dangerous time. A twelve year old girl and two other teens recently bought a single

---

[1] Bishop Robert Barron, *"Go on a Hero's Journey - Bishop Barron's Sunday Sermon,"* August 6, 2022, video, accessed August 7, 2022, https://youtu.be/V5lI3xYWE1w.

fentanyl pill in Santa Clara County. The twelve year old passed out and died a short time later. Now more than ever, Jesus is calling you to relationship with Him.

I believe that Jesus is calling you to stand in the gap, to fight for your brothers and sisters. In fact, I believe that He is calling you to do more than overcome the problems above. He is calling you to save the souls of your generation. When you develop a personal relationship with Jesus, you discover what He is calling you to do, and He always calls you to Mission. He calls you from the comfort of your life, from what is easy and familiar; He leads you into battle against the enemy with the power of His grace. He calls you into quite an adventure ... a mission to fight the giants of darkness in today's world.

What do I mean by this? Consider the example of Bilbo Baggins from *The Hobbit*. As the story begins, Bilbo Baggins, like the other hobbits, is comfortable and complacent. He enjoys his creature comforts, and he is happy with his snug little hole at Bag End in the Shire. Nevertheless, the wizard Gandalf believes that there is much more to Bilbo, much more than you can see on the surface.

Gandalf recruits Bilbo to assist in Thorin's quest for the treasure under the mountain, and Bilbo begins a gradual process of self-development. As the story progresses, Bilbo transforms from a wary hermit to a courageous and self-assured hero. Bilbo slowly becomes the leading force, keeping the group of dwarves together, and he displays leadership qualities that he never knew he had. In Mirkwood, Bilbo saves the dwarves from wood elves and spiders, by shouting for Gandalf, he saves them from the goblins. Bilbo discovers Smaug's weak spot, and he attempts to fight against Thorin's greed. Bilbo's efforts help to bring peace to the fighting elves, dwarves and humans.

Gandalf calls Bilbo to Mission, from the safety and security of his little hole, and Bilbo will never be the same. God is calling you to Mission as well, to fight against His enemies and undertake your own hero's journey. As he lived out his Mission, Bilbo fundamentally changed. The same will be true of you. You will never be the same once you develop this personal relationship with the Creator of the Universe. As one teen put it, there is something fundamentally life-changing about coming face to face with Christ. You will discover strength and courage you never knew you had. *For God did not give us a spirit of cowardice but rather of power and love and self-control.* (2 Timothy 1:7)

You will find that God often calls the young to save His people; this is nothing new. David, one of the greatest figures in the Bible, was called by God at a young age. God often calls young people in their teens or early twenties (Jeremiah, Solomon, Samuel, Blessed Virgin Mary) to fight the enemy against overwhelming odds.

Samuel was called as a boy. Some believe that Jeremiah was between thirteen and sixteen when God first spoke to him (and many believe that he began preaching at the age of twenty). In fact, Jeremiah himself complained to God that he was too young (Jeremiah 1:6)! The Virgin Mary was approximately fourteen when she conceived the Savior of the world! God called the young David to take on the giant Goliath and defeat the Philistines. I believe that God is calling the youth to save society right now, and I believe that Jesus wants you to be part of this! That's why you picked up this book, and that's why you're reading it. If you take part in this battle, you will help to save your brothers and sisters, immensely improve your own relationship with Jesus, and experience a journey you'll never forget.

Is God really calling us to battle? What would indicate this?

Go back to the very beginning, to the Garden of Eden, and you'll see what I mean. As the Bible begins, we see Satan entering the Garden, seeking to tempt Adam and Eve, looking for a fight. God could have prevented Satan from entering the Garden, but He did not. He allowed it, because He wants us to fight Satan, His greatest enemy. He also gives us free will and He asks us to make a choice, for or against Him. God gave them the grace to fight, to stand up to Satan. God wanted Adam to embrace his manhood and protect Eve, and He wanted Eve to reject Satan's advances. We all know what happened. They refused to fight, and the human race has suffered terribly ever since, experiencing the misery of sin and corruption down through the ages.

Fast forward many years later to October 13, 1884. After saying his morning mass, Pope Leo XIII suffered a strange and unexplained illness, collapsing on the altar. The faithful in attendance believed that he was dead. After regaining consciousness, the Pope described an unbelievable, terrifying conversation that he overheard while unconscious, a conversation between Jesus and Satan. Satan bragged that he could destroy the Church within seventy-five (or one hundred years, by some accounts), if Jesus would allow him to carry out his plans. Satan also requested "a greater influence over those who will give themselves to my service." Jesus reportedly responded, "you will be given the time and the power." Once again, God allowed Satan to engage in combat with the human race. Jesus knew that with His grace, we could overcome Satan and be victorious. Nevertheless, God once again allowed this battle to take place. Furthermore, to obtain victory, Jesus requires that we be willing to fight.

After this frightening conversation, the Pope was visibly shaken. In response, he composed a special prayer, the *Saint Michael prayer*, and he ordered that it be prayed after Mass. Many churches have continued this practice. The Saint Michael prayer was an immediate result of this conversation between Jesus and Satan. Michael is the angel named in Revelations 12:7 who fought in the battle against Satan, expelling him from Heaven. In the first line of this prayer, Pope Leo XIII asks Saint Michael directly ... to assist us *in battle*.

Saint Michael the Archangel, defend us in the battle; be our defense against the wickedness and snares of the devil. May God rebuke him and do you, O Prince of the Heavenly Host, by the power of God, thrust into hell Satan and the other evil spirits who prowl about the world seeking the ruin of souls. Amen

The book cover attempts to capture something of this famous scene from Revelations 12. As Revelations 12 states, the red dragon is the devil himself. The book cover pictures a famous saint, well known for his battles against Satan, Saint Padre Pio, who bore the wounds of Christ upon his body, the stigmata. Padre Pio is a perfect example of someone who took up the call to fight against the dragon, and with God's grace, won many victories. Padre Pio is credited with performing many miracles, and I cover him briefly in the book. He is a humble example of a warrior, the spiritual warrior that each of us is called to be.

Revelations 12:17 goes on to describe the battle that follows after Satan is expelled from Heaven.

Then the dragon became angry with the woman and went off to wage war against the rest of her offspring, those who keep God's commandments and bear witness to Jesus.

(Revelations 12:17)

Satan wages war against anyone who strives to keep God's commandments and bear witness to Jesus. If you look around you today, it's not difficult to see the effects of this war, and the damage that has occurred. The effects are all around us. With God's grace, a strong prayer life and a personal relationship with Jesus, you can fight Satan and inflict casualties and losses upon the forces of evil.

The results of this battle, begun in the Garden of Eden and continuing to our present day, are eternal. The rewards for fighting this battle are also eternal. Some rewards are temporary, and some are eternal. By God's grace, I have won trophies for soccer games played in my youth. There is nothing wrong with these trophies, but they are gathering dust, sitting on my mantle, forgotten. The rewards for this cosmic struggle, however, last forever. No matter what you achieve in life, you will find that the honors of this world never last. Furthermore, nothing compares with the achievement of helping to save a soul from Hell for all eternity. Try to imagine the gratitude of such a soul, if you can. What would it be like to meet them in Heaven?!

Catholicism and Christianity are a TEAM SPORT. We are all in this fight together, by design. My prayers and your prayers ... my actions and your actions ... are directly instrumental in saving our brothers and sisters, our fellow team-mates. This is called the Communion of Saints, and its consequences reach beyond time and space; its consequences reach beyond the grave and echo into eternity. In the Church approved apparitions of Fatima, the Virgin Mary said that many souls go to hell because they have no one to make sacrifices or pray for them. Your prayers and sacrifices can make the difference ... eternally.

I believe that God has created us with a desire for the Hero's journey; I believe that He has wired this into our very being. This is why superhero movies are so successful. Deep down, we want to be a Hero ... we want to fight for victory ... we want to take Satan down ... we want to save our brothers and sisters.

How do we succeed in this battle?

We succeed with God's help! We seek this help by requesting it from Him and by establishing a personal relationship with Him. One powerful way of doing this, recommended by the Blessed Mother herself, is by praying the Rosary. This book presents many short stories of the power of the Rosary, illustrating how this prayer has overcome evil. You will see how the Rosary saved John in the World Trade Center on 9/11, how it saved a young woman from a serial killer, and how it saved a Satanic priest from Satan. You will find these stories to be interesting and entertaining, and they will inspire you to pick up the Rosary.

In addition, Jesus has made it clear that He wants us to speak with Him in our own words, in a one on one conversation. You read that correctly. Jesus wants to speak with you one on one. Psalm 95:7 says ... *if today you hear His voice.* Why would it say this unless you could actually hear His voice (not necessarily audibly)? This type of prayer, conversational prayer, is distinguished from the Rosary by the fact that it is entirely in your own words. You will sit and converse with Jesus as you sit and talk to a friend. The saints have strongly recommended this type of prayer and have highly praised the blessings it provides. Jesus, being a personal God, wants to talk to you personally. I can't emphasize this enough. In addition, I can't begin to guess what He might say to you, but I'm sure that it's a conversation you don't want to miss. I cover conversational prayer in the final section of the book. Keep in mind that there is no getting around the following point: Prayer is critical in our personal relationship with Jesus and the battle He is calling us to fight. I'm not going to sugar-coat this in the least. However, Jesus never forces anyone to pray. In the quote at the beginning of this section, Jesus says that He stands at the door and knocks. He knocks at the door of your life, hoping you will open the door to him by communicating with Him through PRAYER.

Through the Rosary and conversational prayer, you will hear what Jesus wants of you, learn why He gave you your particular talents and abilities, and you will undertake the Hero's journey He is calling you to make.

You will help save the souls of your brothers and sisters and God-willing, enjoy the eternal reward of your efforts. Know too that I am fighting this fight, practicing what I preach, hoping to find my own part in the victory. I provide details in the Warriors For Mary section.

Before going further, I don't want to take anything for granted. How do we know that Jesus is Real ... that Catholicism and Christianity are Real? Personally, I benefit from scientific evidence in this regard. I do not base my faith on scientific evidence alone; scientific evidence provides additional proof to help me believe. Scientific evidence allows me to see that my faith does not go against reason. The revelation of truth in the Church is well founded, but our limited minds often want additional evidence. Jesus was perfectly willing to perform miracles two thousand years ago to support our faith, and He is willing to do so again today. I want to give you confidence that Christianity and Catholicism are Real. I want you to see that there is solid evidence for the faith. I provide this evidence next with the Big Three.

INTRODUCING THE *BIG THREE*: SCIENTIFICALLY ANALYZED EVIDENCE FOR THE FAITH

Before presenting the Rosary, I present scientifically analyzed evidence for Christianity in general and Catholicism in particular. How do we know Jesus is Real? How do we know Christianity is Real? How do we even know that God is Real? These are important fundamental questions. For those asking these questions, I can confidently tell you that there is significant evidence, complete with scientific analysis and observable physical items, which strongly support Christianity. What is this evidence? Here I concentrate on what I call the *Big Three*: The *Shroud of Turin* (what many believe to be Jesus' burial cloth), *Eucharistic Miracles* and the *tilma* (or jacket) of Juan Diego from the apparitions of Our Lady of Guadalupe. Each provides diligently analyzed scientific evidence supporting the faith. Each helps us to see that the Catholic faith is Real … Christianity is Real; we serve a God who is Real, and we pray to the Man-God, Jesus Christ, who is Real. There is much more evidence for the faith, but I concentrate on these three examples.

After presenting the Big Three, I will use them in Rosary meditations when I present the mysteries of the Rosary. We will see that the Shroud of Turin in particular provides a lot of material for meditation. I provide details on the Big Three below.

In "**Example #1: Scientifically Analyzed Shroud of Turin: A Photo of the Crucified Christ**?" we investigate the findings of numerous scientists from around the world, scientists who have analyzed what may be the burial cloth of Christ. In "**Example #2: Scientifically Analyzed Eucharistic Miracles**," we discover well-known scientists studying Hosts that have changed into human heart tissue! These miracles have occurred recently in Argentina, Poland and Mexico, and they have been approved by the Catholic Church. In "**Example #3: Scientifically Analyzed Tilma from the Apparitions of Our Lady of Guadalupe**," we will look at a miraculous image of the Blessed Mother. This beautiful, colorful image has been meticulously studied by a variety of scientists, and it is full of mysteries and wonders. How it remains intact to this day, more than four centuries after it originally appeared, is itself a mystery.

An artist's rendering of the Resurrection.

EXAMPLE #1: Scientifically Analyzed Shroud of Turin: A Photo of the Crucified Christ?

It is just unbelievable what forensic scientists can tell us ... unbelievable. They have solved cases, found murderers, discovered the cause of serious illnesses and cracked the code on a "cipher," a secret code released by a killer. My hat is off to forensic scientists. They are able to find answers in what appear to be random circumstances. By combining knowledge from different disciplines, they find critical facts where you least expect them. They find facts that rise to the level of court admissible evidence. To be court admissible, your facts must have something to them, to put it lightly. Not only are forensic achievements unbelievable, they are also popular in Hollywood, given the current success of shows like *Forensic Files*. After watching my first episode of *Forensic Files*, I had a hard time stopping. As you will see, forensic science can do more than find murderers and solve crimes. It can help solve the mystery of the most studied artifact in the history of the world[2]–the Shroud of Turin. Is this the burial cloth of Christ? Is this a photograph of the crucified God-Man?

---

[2] Mark Niyr, *The Turin Shroud: Physical Evidence of Life After Death?* (Morgan Hill, CA: Bookstand Publishing, 2020), 14.

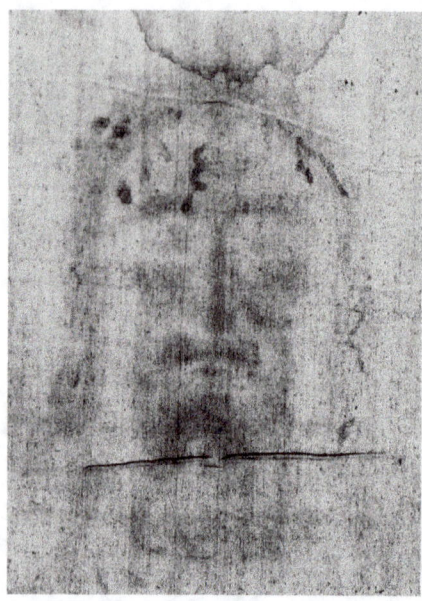

Photographic positive is shown on the left and photographic negative on the right. The photos above display a partial view of the front of the Shroud, showing the bloodied and swollen face of a crucified man. © Vernon Miller, 1978. No unauthorized reproduction of Material on other Websites is allowed without prior written permission from the shroudphotos.com copyright holder. Original photos are available for free at shroudphotos.com.

What is the Shroud and Why is it Important?

The Shroud of Turin is a linen cloth believed by many to be the burial cloth of Jesus. This cloth shows the image of a crucified man, with wounds to the wrists, feet, face, head and side and numerous scourge marks. The Shroud measures fourteen feet three inches long by three feet seven inches wide, long enough to cover the front and back of a deceased man. The wounds on the cloth correspond with the Gospel accounts of the crucifixion of Jesus.

In 1898, the very first photograph of the Shroud was taken by an amateur Italian photographer, Secondo Pia. Pia next developed the image, and he was astonished at what he saw. From his negative emerged the clearly discernible face of a man, badly beaten, with wounds on his cheeks and forehead. The negative also showed what appears to be a crucified body, with scourges, shoulder wounds, pierced wrists, pierced feet and blood flowing from a pierced side. In Secondo Pia's negative, the features of the Man of the Shroud were now clearly visible. The positive image of the Shroud, pictured above, is much less distinct, and it is difficult to discern the details without viewing the negative.

Why is the Shroud important? There are many reasons, but I will focus on three. First, this cloth may provide physical evidence of Jesus' Resurrection. This is clearly of great importance, as the Resurrection is the central teaching of Christianity. Second, the Shroud may provide physical evidence of what Jesus actually suffered during His crucifixion. This is critical to understanding what Jesus went through to win our salvation. Third, the Shroud may provide a photo of what Jesus actually looked like. Using the face on the Shroud, artists have attempted to recreate a portrait of Jesus. The Italian police have created a picture of Jesus, using age regression software, to determine what He may have looked like at age twelve. Being human, we have a need to see the face of Jesus, to gain some idea of how he looked. The face on the Shroud bridges the distance of space and time, allowing us to see what may be a photo of Jesus captured for our generation to discover two thousand years later. Suddenly, Jesus' life and words, His death and His crucifixion, become much more tangible, much more real.

As noted, the Shroud is the most studied article in the history of the world. Scientific tests, studies, examinations, what-if analyses, chemical analyses, recreation attempts—you name it—all of these and more have been performed on the Shroud. Physicists, chemists, biologists, archaeologists, forensic palynologists—a vast array of some of the world's greatest scientists, using some of the world's most advanced scientific equipment–have examined and tested the Shroud. Forensic science, with its current technological advances, has been applied, particularly in the areas of blood, pollen and limestone. The findings are nothing short of amazing. After studying this topic, it is clear to me that scientific analysis of the Shroud is well established, and many of the findings have been summarized in peer-reviewed journals. I believe that the evidence for the authenticity of the Shroud is well documented, but you will have to judge for yourself.

Study of the Shroud is ongoing, and full coverage of this topic is beyond the scope of this book. However, I summarize some of the main findings below. I first cover the 1988 carbon-14 dating; carbon-14 dating alleged that the Shroud originated between 1260 and 1390, suggesting that it was the work of a medieval forger.

1988 Carbon Dating[3]

(Please keep in mind that more recent tests have dated the Shroud to within the time of Christ). In 1988, three different labs used carbon-14 dating to independently date the Shroud. A sample was cut from the Shroud, and the labs produced dates ranging from 1260-1390 AD, centuries after Jesus was crucified. Many in the media concluded that the Shroud was a fake, the work of a creative medieval forger working in the thirteenth century. They believed that these results settled the question for good. However, the media disregarded very significant facts about carbon dating.

Carbon dating is not conclusive, although this fact is not very well known by the public; carbon dating can be seriously hampered by sample contamination. In fact, field archaeologists and geologists generally view sample contamination as a serious problem with carbon-14 dating. As Mark Niyr points out, living snail shells have been dated as twenty-six thousand years old, and a seal was dated as thirteen hundred years old just after it had been killed. Another carbon-14 test dated a Viking horn

---

[3] Niyr, *The Turin Shroud: Physical Evidence of Life After Death?*, 65-68.

as eighteen years in the future. Obviously, carbon-14 dating can produce inaccurate results. When performing the 1988 tests on the Shroud, the labs used a sample cut from the top left-hand corner. This is undoubtedly one of the most contaminated parts of the Shroud, since this corner was touched each time someone picked it up.

Another problem with the 1988 carbon-14 test was the limited number of labs performing the testing. In 1988, the Shroud custodian made a last-minute decision to limit the testing to three labs, rather than the seven originally planned. Each of the three labs performing the testing signed a protest letter noting that they would be irresponsible if they did not point out that this very significant modification in the proposed testing procedures could lead to failure. Therefore, even the labs themselves warned of the possibility of erroneous results! In addition, a report published in *Science News* expressed "grave concern" over the new accelerator technology that was used to test the Shroud.

Another carbon-14 dating test, an unauthorized test, was performed in 1982 on a thread taken from the Shroud known as the Raes-sample. This sample was tested at the nuclear accelerator facility of the University of California. One end of thread was dated to 200 AD, while the other end of the thread, contaminated with starch, was dated to 1000 AD. In general, the media reported the 1988 carbon-14 results as conclusive, without mentioning these other findings.

More Recent Dating[4]

Nearly three decades later, more state-of-the-art tests have dated the Shroud to within the time of Christ. In June 2015, Padua University in Italy convened a scientific conference entitled: "Workshop of Paduan Scientific Analysis on the Shroud." This scientific conference announced the results obtained from Padua University, working in collaboration with other European universities. They reported the following regarding their summary of the 1988 carbon-14 dating: After the 1988 radiocarbon dating result was not found to be statistically reliable, probably due to environmental pollution, other methods demonstrated that the age of the Shroud is compatible with the time that Jesus lived and died in Palestine.

The scientists used other methods to date the Shroud, methods based on chemical and mechanical tests, using more current technology. Professor Giulio Fanti (who headed the Shroud Science Group of approximately 140 scientists), Fabio Crosilla and Pierandrea Malfi wrote an abstract summarizing their findings. They determined that these new dating methods dated the Shroud to 90 AD, plus or minus 200 years, with a 95% confidence level. They pointed out that their new dating results contradict the date range found by the 1988 radiocarbon testing, conducted almost 30 years earlier.

---

[4] Niyr, *The Turin Shroud: Physical Evidence of Life After Death?*, 68-69.

The Shroud of Turin Research Project[5]

Ten years before the carbon-14 dating tests were performed, in October 1978, a team of twenty-five specialists and scientists from around the world visited Turin to study the Shroud. This project was named the Shroud of Turin Research Project, or STURP. Eventually, the team grew to a total of 33 international members, representing a variety of scientific disciplines and bearing credentials from twenty major research institutions. The team brought seven tons of scientific equipment with them. After two years of preparation, the team spent five full days studying the Shroud, performing advanced tests such as photographic floodlighting, low X-rays, and narrow-band ultraviolet lighting.

Many on the team believed that they could quickly debunk the Shroud's image as artistic forgery. They believed that they would find painting, sketching or some other indication that this was the work of a medieval artist. However, many unusual findings came to light, findings that had lain hidden for two thousand years.

In the final paragraph of their report, STURP concluded that the Shroud image shows the true human form of a crucified man, and it is not the creation of an artist. The bloodstains contain hemoglobin and give positive results

---

[5] Gerard Verschuuren, *A Catholic Scientist Champions the Shroud of Turin* (Manchester, NH: Sophia Institute Press, 2021), 56-57; Niyr, *The Turin Shroud: Physical Evidence of Life After Death?*, 16.

for serum albumin. STURP notes that the image remains a mystery, which remains unsolved, until a group of scientists in the future can provide further chemical studies.

STURP concluded that this was not the work of an artist. Below, I consider additional findings that shed light on this question. Using a combination of questioning and forensic evidence, I believe that we can go a long way toward discovering the origin of the Shroud. What does the current evidence have to say?

Unusual Photographic Characteristics of the Shroud

When considering the authenticity of the Shroud, perhaps the first topic to address is its unusual photographic characteristics. As pictured above, the Shroud is actually a photographic negative. After photographing the Shroud in 1898, Secondo Pia developed a negative of the positive, and he was shocked, almost dropping the negative plate.[6] Unlike the rather blurry image visible in the positive, the negative showed much greater detail, illustrating what appeared to be a photograph of a crucified man. The image on the Shroud bore the characteristics of a photographic negative, which when photographed, produced a positive-like photographic image on the negative plate. Is it possible to counterfeit

---

[6] Niyr, *The Turin Shroud: Physical Evidence of Life After Death?*, 23.

such an effect? How could someone create such an effect five hundred years before the invention of the camera? Why would someone bother to produce details that no one in their century would ever see or understand? In fact, there's more. This forger went far beyond photographic concepts; in fact, his ability was rather impressive even from a twenty-first century standpoint! The forger produced a three-dimensional image ... on a two-dimensional cloth![7]

A Three-Dimensional Image on a Two-Dimensional Cloth

Physicist John Jackson, who led the Unites States team of scientists at STURP, and Bill Motten, an image specialist from Sandia Laboratory, conducted a test at Sandia Laboratory using a VP-8 Image Analyzer, a tool used to simulate three-dimensional elevations. The results were stunning; the Shroud gave off a three-dimensional display of its image, correctly proportioned![8]

As Jackson and Motten viewed the Shroud using the Image Analyzer, they inspected the three-dimensional form, exploring its heights and depths. How could someone create a three-dimensional image on linen?

---

[7] Niyr, *The Turin Shroud: Physical Evidence of Life After Death?*, 36; Verschuuren, *A Catholic Scientist Champions the Shroud of Turin*, 55.
[8] Niyr, *The Turin Shroud: Physical Evidence of Life After Death?*, 36.

Peter Schumacher, an engineer who pioneered the production of the VP-8 Image Analyzer, delivered a paper to the Shroud of Turin International Research Conference in Richmond, Virginia. He made the following observations.[9] The VP-8 Analyzer produced a true three-dimensional image on the monitor, a result that had not occurred with any of the images he had investigated. Furthermore, he had never heard of this result occurring in image studies performed by anyone else. The results were unlike anything he had ever seen through the VP-8 Analyzer, before or since.

Schumacher raised several questions. How could an artist control the quality of the work when he could not see three-dimensional information? Why wouldn't an artist share this new technique with other artists from his time period? One would expect to see this effect in other works of art.

Lest anyone conclude that the VP-8 Image Analyzer conferred three-dimensional properties onto the Shroud, Peter Schumacher added that the VP-8 Image Analyzer does not create the three-dimensional result; the Shroud image creates this result. Furthermore, the Shroud is the only image known to induce such a result.

Using this three-dimensional information embedded in the Shroud image, Jackson and his colleague Eric Jumper

---

[9] Niyr, *The Turin Shroud: Physical Evidence of Life After Death?*, 37.

created a three-dimensional map of the body of the Man of the Shroud. They discovered that the cloth itself contains distance data, information that has somehow been placed within the image. For cloth to convey distance information, the Man of the Shroud must have been wrapped within this cloth at some point. The three-dimensional information within the Shroud communicates the distance between the cloth and body at every point.

I next turn to another source of evidence on the Shroud's authenticity, pollen samples. Pollen samples have been used extensively in forensic research, helping to locate the geographical origins of an object. Pollen evidence has been presented in courts of law, both within the United States and other countries, to prove or disprove a connection in a criminal case. Unsusceptible to decay, pollen spores remain well-preserved for millions of years,[10] making them an excellent source of information in the study of historical objects.

This photo is a photographic negative showing a partial view of the front of the Shroud. © Vernon Miller, 1978. No unauthorized reproduction of Material on other Websites is allowed without prior written permission from the shroudphotos.com copyright holder. Original photos are available for free at shroudphotos.com.

---

[10] John Jackson and the Turin Shroud Center of Colorado, *The Shroud of Turin: A Critical Summary of Observations, Data and Hypotheses* (Colorado Springs: The Turin Shroud Center of Colorado, 2017), 63.

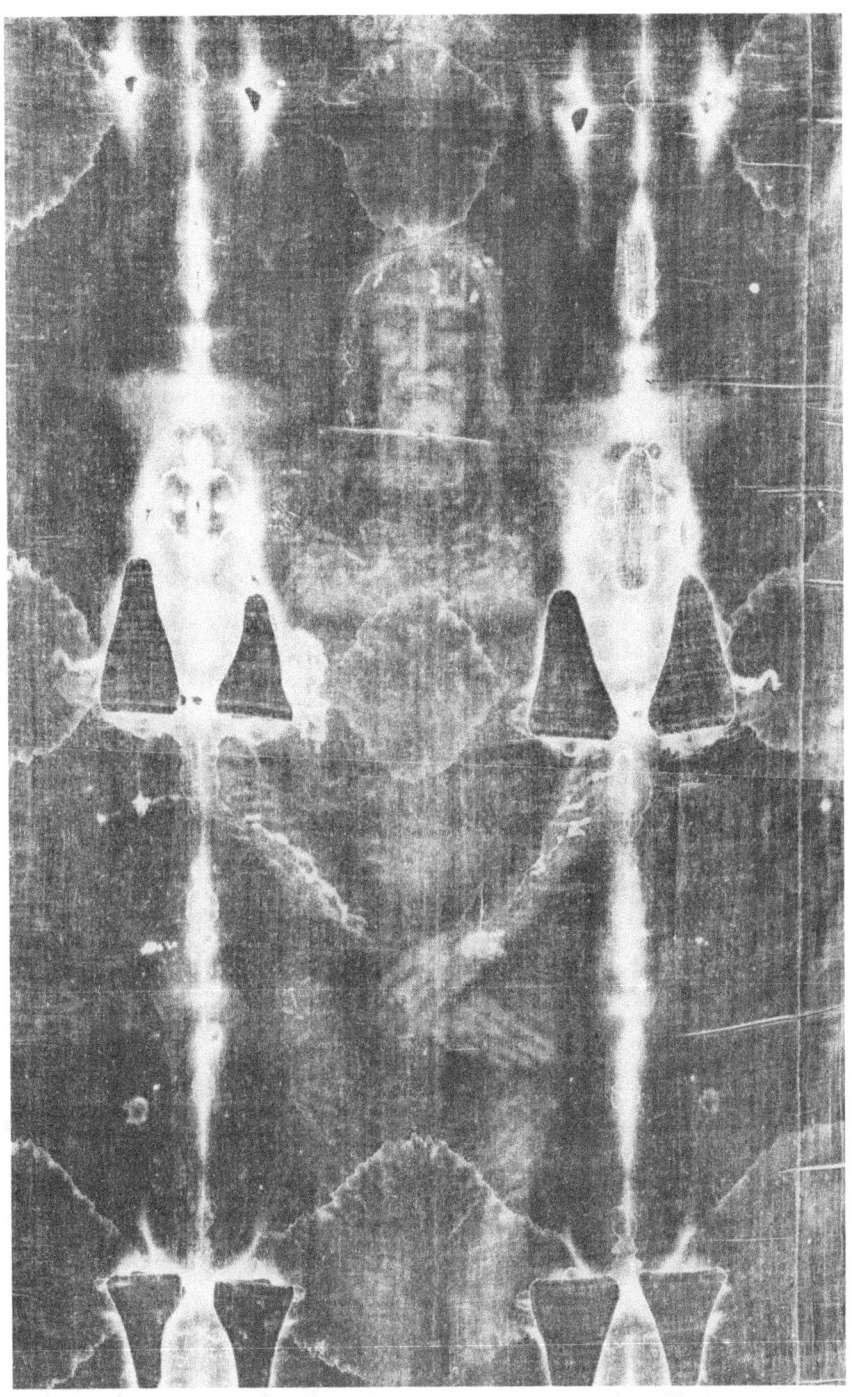

Pollen from Plants in Jerusalem on the Shroud[11]

During the STURP investigations, Dr. Max Frei, an internationally acclaimed criminologist and botanist, studied pollen grains present on the Shroud. During his lifetime, Max Frei was recognized as one of the leading criminal forensic scientists in Europe, founding the Central Police Scientific Department in Zurich, Switzerland, where he oversaw forensic scientific studies. Max Frei led the STURP effort to determine the geographical details of the Shroud, including places it had been during its history.

As noted, pollen has been used in court cases, sometimes providing the vital clues necessary to solve a murder. Max Frei often used pollen to help solve crimes. The power of pollen samples rests upon several important facts. Pollen grains are extremely small, invisible to the naked eye. In order to distinguish one type from another, you need a Scanning Electron Microscope (SEM); thus, it is difficult to hide the presence of pollen grains, for the simple reason that you can't see them. Second, every geographical area on earth has its own unique pollen grains, released from the particular variety of plants that grow there. Since pollen grains can remain for millions of years, they provide a lasting fingerprint for a region. Finally, pollen grains adhere to

---

[11] Jackson and the Turin Shroud Center of Colorado, *The Shroud of Turin: A Critical Summary of Observations, Data and Hypotheses*, 62-64; Niyr, *The Turin Shroud: Physical Evidence of Life After Death?*, 54-55.

almost any material, such as a linen cloth. For all of these reasons, pollen can provide powerful clues regarding the historical whereabouts of the Shroud.

In November 1973, Frei collected twelve sticky tape samples from the Shroud, and he found pollen from fifty some species of plants. Frei later made seven trips to locations in Palestine, Turkey, France and Italy to obtain additional pollen samples for comparison. Frei performed some of his work using low-powered optical or light microscopic instruments, and some have suggested that he should have used the Scanning Electron Microscope alone. Nevertheless, Frei published an article in the special interest journal *Shroud Spectrum* in June 1982. Frei made the preliminary conclusion that the pollen spectrum confirms the following theory: the Shroud of Turin moved from Palestine through Anatolia, or Turkey, to Constantinople, France and Italy. In fact, the majority of the pollen species found by Frei on the Shroud grow in the vicinity of Jerusalem.

The French scientist Gérard Lucotte studied a sticky tape sample from the nose of the man of the Shroud, and he also found the presence of pollen. Using the Scanning Electron Microscope, Lucotte believed that he found pollen from two species of plants, including Caratonia siliqua (the carob tree) and Balanites aegypiaca (the Judas tree). Each of these are commonly found in Palestine.

Some have argued that pollen could have blown from Jerusalem to Europe, eventually landing on the Shroud. Werner Bulst, S.J., has considered this question.[12] Bulst rejects this argument, noting that it would be a miracle if winds carried more pollen from the East than from the European environment, adding that, due to the different blooming seasons of the associated plants, this same unlikely miracle would have to have been repeated during different seasons of the year.

Limestone from Jerusalem[13]

A member of the STURP team provided sticky tape samples to Dr. Joseph Kohlbeck, a crystallography scientist working at Hercules Aerospace in Utah, and Dr. Kohlbeck discovered calcium carbonate, or limestone, on the tapes originating from the foot area of the Shroud. This was a significant find, as limestone crystals can often provide a geographic signature of a particular location. After making his discovery, Kohlbeck contacted a Utah archaeologist, Dr. Eugenia Nitkowski, who conducted research on Israel's rolling stone tombs. Dr. Nitkowski then provided Kohlbeck with samples of Jerusalem limestone from the tombs.

---

[12] Werner Bulst, "The Pollen Grains on the Shroud of Turin," *Shroud Spectrum International* 3, no. 10 (March 1984): 25-26.

[13] Mark Antonacci, *The Resurrection of the Shroud* (New York: M. Evans and Company, 2000), 109; Jackson and the Turin Shroud Center of Colorado, *The Shroud of Turin: A Critical Summary of Observations, Data and Hypotheses,* 61-62; Cheryl Leonard, *The Shroud of Turin: The Scientific Evidence* (2015), 6-9.

After further analysis, Kohlbeck concluded that the Shroud limestone and tomb limestone were both Travertine Aragonite, a rare type of limestone found in Jerusalem and several other locations. The Shroud limestone appeared to match the tomb limestone very closely, and both contained small amounts of strontium and iron. Kohlbeck decided to seek further confirmation.

Kohlbeck brought both samples to Dr. Ricardo Levi-Setti of the University of Chicago's Enrico Fermi Institute. Using a high resolution scanning ion microprobe, Levi-Setti studied the wavelengths emitted from the two limestone samples, and he confirmed that they were an unusually close match. Minute pieces of flax could not be separated from the Shroud sample (linen is made from flax), and this caused a slight variation. Levi-Setti also analyzed limestone samples taken from nine different test sites in Israel, but he discovered a match only when comparing against the limestone taken from the Jerusalem tomb.

Could all of this be a coincidence? Could Travertine Aragonite limestone have somehow found its way onto the Shroud?

Human Blood Found on the Shroud and its Unusual Characteristics: *Why would it remain red?*

For Barrie Schwortz, STURP photographer, this was the clue that tipped the scales; this was the finding that led him to believe that the Shroud is truly authentic.[14] In a moment, hopefully you will understand why.

By way of background, Schwortz was raised a Conservative Jew, and he embraced Conservative Judaism until the age of about thirteen. He then left the faith. Later, he was asked to be the technical photographer for the STURP project conducted in 1978, and he reluctantly accepted the job. Although he did not consider himself to be a practicing Jew, he still felt that (1) the Shroud was probably a fake and (2) he had no particular attraction to Christianity. Thus, he remained a skeptic for years before accepting the Shroud as authentic. He was perplexed at the color of the blood on the Shroud; why was it red rather than dark brown? Dark brown is the color one would expect from dried human blood. The answer to this question is rather amazing; for Schwortz, it made all the difference.

Before I explain this, I want to note that the blood on the Shroud is in fact real human blood.[15] In addition, Dr. Baima Ballone and colleagues determined that the blood type is type AB.[16] This becomes even more

---

[14] Barrie Schwortz, "*The Shroud and the Jew: Barrie Schwortz at TEDx ViadellaConciliazione,*" TEDx Talks, May 1, 2013, video, 7:00, accessed November 14, 2021, https://youtu.be/4G4sj8hUVaY.

[15] Jackson and the Turin Shroud Center of Colorado, *The Shroud of Turin: A Critical Summary of Observations, Data and Hypotheses,* 53; Niyr, *The Turin Shroud: Physical Evidence of Life After Death?,* 31; Antonacci, *The Resurrection of the Shroud,* 28.

[16] Antonacci, *The Resurrection of the Shroud,* 28.

interesting when we consider that this matches the blood type discovered in Eucharistic Miracles; the blood type in Eucharistic Miracle heart tissue is also type AB! (I cover Eucharistic Miracles below.) This blood type is not very common; three percent of the world possesses blood type AB, and a disproportionate percentage of the Jewish population (18%) possesses this blood type.[17] (When considering the Shroud blood type, Kelly Kearse concluded that the preponderance of current scientific evidence indicates it is most likely type AB[18]).

Returning to Barrie Schwortz, the blood on the Shroud has another very peculiar characteristic that helps to explain its color. The blood on the Shroud has a high content of a substance known as bilirubin. Why is this important? Bilirubin is produced in large quantities in the case of violent deaths. During a violent death, a victim experiences traumatic shock which leads to hemolysis, where hemoglobin is released into surrounding fluid. This type of blood has a richer and redder color, and it picks up high levels of bilirubin as it passes through the liver.[19] Thus, after a violent crucifixion, we would expect Jesus' blood to retain a red color as it dried. This is what we would expect from a man who was severely scourged, beaten and crucified.

---

[17] Niyr, *The Turin Shroud: Physical Evidence of Life After Death?*, 31.
[18] Kelly Kearse, "Blood on the Shroud of Turin: An Immunological Review," Shroud of Turin Website (2012): 16, accessed September 11, 2021, https://www.shroud.com/pdfs/kearse.pdf.
[19] Antonacci, *The Resurrection of the Shroud*, 29.

There are many unusual findings related to blood and blood flow on the Shroud, but I will focus on one, Jesus' side wound. Jesus received His side wound when He was pierced by a lance (John 19:34). As John 19:33 notes, the soldiers came to Jesus on the cross and *saw that he was already dead.* After making this determination, one of the soldiers thrust his lance into Jesus' side. Thus, Jesus' side wound is a post-mortem wound, received after His death, and consequently, we would expect this wound to show certain characteristics observable by modern forensic science.

The Shroud shows a side wound between the fifth and sixth ribs on the right side of the chest,[20] with a large amount of blood and fluid pooling under the man's back as he lay in the Shroud.[21] The side wound on the Shroud also shows a blood flow from the right auricle, which would fill with blood after death. Had Jesus been alive when He received this wound, the blood would have splattered from breathing, but the Shroud shows no signs of this; the Shroud shows blood flowing out by gravity, without being propelled by a beating heart. This blood flow shows no sign of breathing or heartbeat, indicating that the wound was received after death.[22] In addition, there is no swelling seen with the side wound.[23] As Jackson notes, the preponderance of forensic evidence supports

---

[20] Niyr, *The Turin Shroud: Physical Evidence of Life After Death?*, 47.
[21] Jackson and the Turin Shroud Center of Colorado, *The Shroud of Turin: A Critical Summary of Observations, Data and Hypotheses,* 52.
[22] Niyr, *The Turin Shroud: Physical Evidence of Life After Death?*, 31.
[23] Antonacci, *The Resurrection of the Shroud,* 20.

the conclusion that the side wound was post-mortem.[24] Did a forger anticipate all of these things when he faked the side wound?

There is much more that I could say about the Shroud, its scientific analysis, how blood flow on the Shroud correctly matches what we would expect anatomically, given the force of gravity and the angle at which Jesus hung on the cross. However, I would like to move on to my main point, the question most people are asking … what is the image on the Shroud, and how was it created? As noted, linen is not a photographic medium by any means, so how was the image created?

Before covering this, I would like to emphasize the following: to fake the Shroud, a forger would need to (1) depict human blood with all of the correct characteristics; (2) avoid the use of paint; (3) provide for environmental factors such as dirt or limestone; (4) provide for environmental factors such as pollen grains, invisible to the naked eye; (5) understand photographic positive and negative images; (6) understand how to correctly encode three-dimensional information into an image; and (7) correctly depict blood flow, accounting for angles, post-mortem wounds, and details only visible with an electron microscope. (This is not an exhaustive list.) To crown this amazing achievement, the forger would have to depict all of the above … in a photographic-like image on linen.

---

[24] Jackson and the Turin Shroud Center of Colorado, *The Shroud of Turin: A Critical Summary of Observations, Data and Hypotheses*, 52.

The Image on the Shroud: *How was it Created, and Does it Provide Evidence of the Resurrection?*

Please note that this is a subject of ongoing scientific research, so you will need to search the Internet for the latest. YouTube provides quite a bit of material on this subject.

As noted, linen is not a photographic medium. Let's take a closer look at the image itself, its color and its depth, also known as its superficiality, to better understand what may have created it. Superficiality measures how deeply the image is imprinted onto the Shroud. Does it appear primarily on the surface of the cloth, or does it penetrate deeper?

Scientists were surprised to find that the image is exceedingly superficial. To get some idea, consider the following. A single linen thread is composed of many small thread fibers, and these are often too small to be seen by the naked eye; thread fibers are ten to twenty times smaller than a human hair. Wherever the image appears on the Shroud, it only appears on the top two or three fibers![25] The straw yellow color of the image only penetrates to 0.2 microns, or about 0.000008 of an inch! Another surprising discovery is that this superficiality of color is consistent throughout the entire Shroud image.[26]

---

[25] Niyr, *The Turin Shroud: Physical Evidence of Life After Death?*, 41.
[26] Niyr, *The Turin Shroud: Physical Evidence of Life After Death?*, 41.

Another unusual feature of the image is that it shows areas that did not directly touch the cloth.[27] Imagine a linen cloth draped over a dead man's body, lying flat on a stone slab. There would be areas of the body that did not have direct contact with the cloth. The eyes, for example, might not touch the cloth as it rested over the eyebrows. Nevertheless, the eyes are still captured in the image on the Shroud.

Dr. John Jackson, the physicist who led the STURP team in 1978, has considered a number of hypotheses on the creation of the Shroud.[28] He rates each in terms of how well it explains the features of the Shroud image. He concludes that there is only one hypothesis that currently meets all of the requirements: the *Radiation Fall-Through Hypothesis.* This hypothesis is named after the process of a man's body becoming "transparent" while the Shroud "falls through" the space formerly occupied by the body! It amazes me that a well-known and well-respected scientist is talking about the Resurrection! Using theoretical modeling, computer simulation and the Shroud as a point of reference, Jackson is essentially studying how the Resurrection might have taken place! Were it not for Dr. Jackson's credentials, publications and impressive achievements, I would be tempted to believe that he was not trustworthy. We are often told that faith and science have nothing to do with one another, that

---

[27] Niyr, *The Turin Shroud: Physical Evidence of Life After Death?*, 42.
[28] Jackson and the Turin Shroud Center of Colorado, *The Shroud of Turin: A Critical Summary of Observations, Data and Hypotheses*, 87.

they contradict one another. However, as Jackson himself states, *"Here, at the tomb of Christ, science and religion are being blended together."*[29]

One final point before I discuss this hypothesis. If Jesus truly rose from the dead as Scripture states, and if the Shroud is truly His burial cloth, we would expect there to be no signs of bodily decay on the Shroud. This is in fact what we find; there are no signs of putrefaction on the Shroud.[30] If the body decayed, we would find signs of decomposition in the nose, mouth or other orifices, or we would find fluid stains indicating this, but none of these have been found on the Shroud. Instead, the Shroud reveals a body still in rigor mortis, with one leg and heel raised up off the ground, a head tilted slightly to the right, and a round behind, which should have flattened from the force of gravity. Rigor mortis only lasts for two or three days. If the Man of the Shroud resurrected, then this period of time would correspond with the Scriptures, which state that Jesus rose on the third day. (1 Corinthians 15:4)

What is Jackson's hypothesis? Jackson believes that the man of the Shroud became radiant with light in the vacuum ultraviolet range (VUV). Simultaneously, the body

---

[29] Jerry Circelli, "Renowned researcher Dr. John Jackson reveals his findings about the Shroud of Turin at SMG talk," *North Texas Catholic*, December 2, 2013, accessed September 12, 2021, Link no longer available.
[30] Jackson and the Turin Shroud Center of Colorado, *The Shroud of Turin: A Critical Summary of Observations, Data and Hypotheses*, 76; Niyr, *The Turin Shroud: Physical Evidence of Life After Death?*, 25.

became "mechanically transparent," no longer occupying physical space. As the body gradually became transparent, it offered less and less resistance to the linen cloth, and the cloth eventually collapsed or "fell through" the space previously occupied by the body, pulled by the force of gravity. The irradiated cloth would then have aged over an unspecified period of time, producing the Shroud image.

To test his hypothesis, Jackson and his team irradiated linen cloths using ultraviolet light, and they heated the linen in an oven to induce the characteristics of aging. Jackson discovered that linen treated in this manner produced a superficial image that closely matched the Shroud image, both visually and chemically.

This hypothesis makes a prediction regarding image characteristics that Jackson later tested. Jackson predicted he would find a "doubly superficial" image on the back of the Shroud, an image similar to the frontal image. As the cloth fell through the man's body, now radiant and transparent, the vacuum ultraviolet light would presumably direct radiation toward the back side of the linen cloth. Amazingly, Jackson's prediction turned out to be true. When Jackson made this prediction, the back side of the Shroud had been covered for centuries. However, during the 2002 preservation project, the "Holland cloth" covering the back side was removed, revealing a very faint superficial image of the face and possibly the hands as well.[31]

---

[31] Jackson and the Turin Shroud Center of Colorado, *The Shroud of Turin: A Critical Summary of Observations, Data and Hypotheses,* 83.

Mark Antonacci endorsed Jackson's hypothesis, but he offered a slight variation, suggesting that the dead man's body produced particle radiation instead of vacuum ultraviolet radiation. In his *Historically Consistent Hypothesis*, Antonacci and his team of scientists suggested that the protons and neutrons found in particle radiation altered the natural qualities of the linen.[32] As the body disappeared, the air between the body and the Shroud would have remained briefly, and particle radiation from the body would have struck the linen cloth. Proton and alpha particles die quickly in air; thus, those parts of the Shroud cloth that were closest to the body would have received the highest number of radiation strikes. As physicist Arthur Lind has observed, there is no body image on the Shroud where more than four inches separate the body from the draped linen Shroud. The area underneath the crossed hands, for example, does not display an image, since the radiation died before it reached this point. Similarly, there is no body image at the mid horizontal sides of the body.

Following the Historically Consistent Hypothesis, every part of the body, including the hair, would have emitted its own particle radiation, doing so in proportion to its distance from the cloth. STURP chemist Dr. John Heller observed that every pore and hair of the body seemed to contain a tiny laser.[33] Antonacci is not alone in proposing

---

[32] Niyr, *The Turin Shroud: Physical Evidence of Life After Death?*, 71-78.
[33] Niyr, *The Turin Shroud: Physical Evidence of Life After Death?*, 76.

that particle radiation produced the Shroud image. Dr. Kitty Little, a retired nuclear physicist who worked at Britain's Atomic Energy Research Establishment, Jean-Baptiste Rinaudo, a biophysicist from the Center for Nuclear Medical Research in Montpellier, France, and Dr. Thomas Phillips, who worked at the High Energy Physics Laboratory at Harvard University, have each theorized that the source of this particle radiation was the body itself![34]

I will mention two final points, the skeletal images recorded on the Shroud and the red color of the blood; both of these lend support to the idea that particle radiation may have caused the image. As noted above, we would expect the blood on the Shroud to be dark brown or black due to its age. Dr. Carlo Goldoni determined that when blood is exposed to neutron radiation followed by ultraviolet light, this causes blood to preserve its red color.[35] Particle radiation could also account for the skeletal images recorded on the Shroud. Scientists have discovered that the Shroud reveals skeletal features, such as bones within the hands and underlying teeth on the right side of the mouth![36] Could linen have passed through a radiant man's body, capturing images of his internal bones ... like an x-ray?

Considering all of the Shroud's characteristics, would it be possible to counterfeit an image like this? In 2000,

---

[34] Niyr, *The Turin Shroud: Physical Evidence of Life After Death?*, 75.
[35] Niyr, *The Turin Shroud: Physical Evidence of Life After Death?*, 76.
[36] Niyr, *The Turin Shroud: Physical Evidence of Life After Death?*, 77.

Antonacci concluded that the image produced on the Shroud could not be reproduced today, even with all of our available technology![37]

A Forger's Possible Motives

Most would agree that a would-be medieval forger would be motivated primarily by financial gain. If the forger could create a convincing counterfeit of Jesus' burial cloth, he would surely receive a large recompense. With this in mind, I consider the following. I do not believe a forger could duplicate the characteristics of the Shroud, but for the sake of argument, let's consider this possibility for a moment. Assuming a forger understood photographic concepts and produced a photographic negative, why would he bother? As you saw above, the image on the Shroud is blurry and difficult to make out. Once Secondo Pia produced the photographic negative, it was far clearer and much more discernible. A thirteenth century audience would never even see the photographic negative, so why would a forger bother to create one? Similarly, a thirteenth century audience would never see three-dimensional information, so why would a forger go to the trouble of creating it? In my opinion, forgery theories need to provide credible motives as well.

---

[37] Antonacci, *The Resurrection of the Shroud*, 213.

Final Point

So Peter and the other disciple went out and came to the tomb. They both ran, but the other disciple ran faster than Peter and arrived at the tomb first; he bent down and saw the burial cloths there, but did not go in. When Simon Peter arrived after him, he went into the tomb and saw the burial cloths there, and the cloth that had covered his head, not with the burial cloths but rolled up in a separate place. Then the other disciple also went in, the one who had arrived at the tomb first, and he saw and believed. For they did not yet understand the scripture that he had to rise from the dead. (John 20:3-9)

My goal in this chapter is to be like Saint John in the Gospel. When John entered the empty tomb, he "saw and believed." The Bible does not say that he saw and forced others to believe; John only acts as a witness to what he has seen. Having studied the evidence available, personally, I believe. I believe that the Shroud is truly the burial cloth of Christ because there is no other plausible explanation for its many characteristics. Keep in mind that modern forensic science has outsmarted some of the best criminal minds in the twenty-first century! I have no doubt that a medieval forger could fool people from his own time; this I do not dispute. However, could a medieval forger fool an audience living six centuries in the future? I do not believe that this is possible. Is the Shroud truly authentic? I leave it to you to decide. The beauty of the Shroud is that it is exceedingly well documented. There is more than enough information available on the Internet for you to explore, and much of it is free. In addition, numerous scientists have published their results in peer-reviewed journals, and these tend to be credible sources of scientific information.

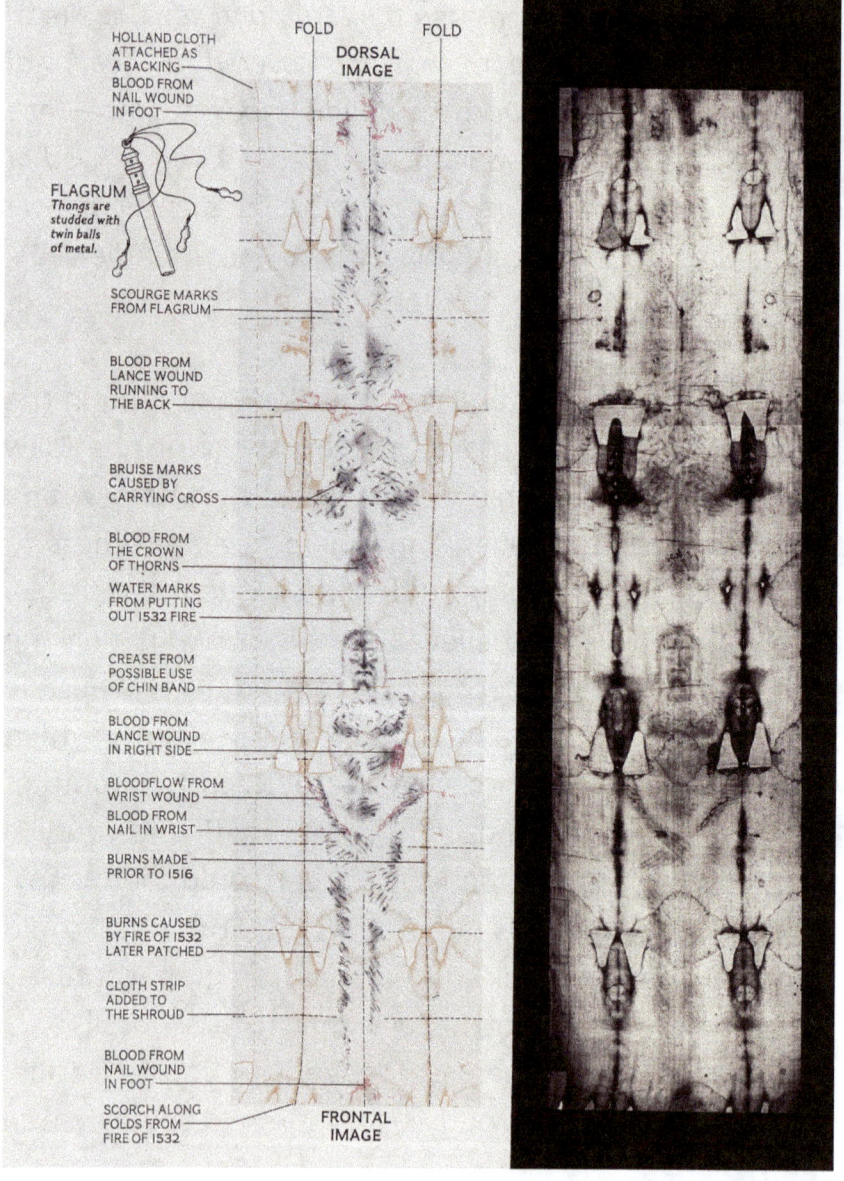

This photo describes the various wounds Jesus received during the Crucifixion, matching them to the corresponding locations on the Shroud. Later, I will include additional information about Jesus' wounds in the Rosary meditations.

EXAMPLE #2: Scientifically Analyzed Eucharistic Miracles

For my flesh is true food, and my blood is true drink.
—Jesus Christ (John 6:55)

Then he said to Thomas, "Put your finger here and see my hands, and bring your hand and put it into my side, and do not be unbelieving, but believe."
—Jesus Christ (John 20:27)

Many of us, like Thomas, are looking for some evidence. Jesus provides physical evidence for us today, just as he did for Thomas. A number of Eucharistic miracles have occurred throughout the world, and I cover several here, focusing on ones that have been scientifically analyzed. By no means do I present them all. There is a Vatican Exhibition of Church-recognized Eucharistic miracles from around the world, and these miracles are recorded in the *Eucharistic Miracles of the World* book. This book covers 152 Eucharistic miracles. The contents of this book have also been placed online (http://therealpresence.org/eucharst/mir/engl_mir.htm), and this website is continually updated as new miracles occur. NOTE: All of the Eucharistic miracles presented here have been accepted by the Catholic Church.

Hosts have changed into living human heart tissue,

which according to modern-day science is impossible. The miracles have led to incredible discoveries about miraculous Hosts concerning blood type, tissue type and the organ that the tissue comes from. When a tissue sample continues living for more than several days, this is something that cannot be explained by modern science. We first consider the Buenos Aires miracle of 1996, which involved the future Pope Francis.

Buenos Aires, Argentina, 1996[38]

It's August 15, 1996 in Buenos Aires. The faithful are receiving Communion. On this particular day, a parishioner of Saint Mary's drops a consecrated Host to the ground. Considering the fallen Host to be "dirty," the parishioner leaves it in the church. Another parishioner, noticing what has happened, picks up the Host and informs the parish priest, Father Alejandro Pezet. Father Alejandro, following standard Church protocol, places the Host in a vessel full of water and then places this vessel into the tabernacle. His purpose is to dissolve the consecrated Host as the Church advises in this situation.

On August 26, Father Alejandro opens the tabernacle to check on the fallen Host, but strangely, the host has not dissolved. In fact, Father Alejandro is amazed to

---

38 Ron Tesoriero, *Reason to Believe: A Personal Story* (Australia: self-pub., 2007), 90-97; Real Presence Eucharistic Education and Adoration Association, *The Eucharistic Miracles of the World: Catalogue of the Vatican International Exhibition*, 2nd ed. (Eternal Life, 2016), 2-7.

see that the Host has developed several reddish stains, and these stains become larger day by day. He informs Cardinal Jorge Bergoglio (Auxiliary Bishop at that time), the future Pope Francis, who instructs that the Host be professionally photographed. The photographs show that the Host, which has become a fragment of bloodied flesh, has grown in size. For several years, the Host is kept in the tabernacle, and the whole affair is kept a strict secret. After seeing that the Host suffers no visible decomposition, Cardinal Bergoglio decides to have it scientifically analyzed.

On October 5, 1999, after Cardinal Bergoglio requested his help, Dr. Castanon takes a sample of the bloody fragment, in the presence of Cardinal Bergoglio's representatives, and sends it to New York for further analysis. Not wishing to prejudice the study, Dr. Castanon does not tell the team of scientists where he obtained the sample. One of the scientists on the team is the well-known cardiologist and forensic pathologist, Dr. Frederic Zugiba (of Columbia University). He determines that the substance is real flesh and blood containing human DNA. As he analyzes the sample, Dr. Zugiba is interviewed by Mike Willesee (television journalist) and Ron Tesoriero (lawyer and cameraman).

Dr. Zugiba notes that the sample seems to be human flesh, with white blood cells and lots of them. He confirms that it is heart tissue from the left ventricle wall, close to the valvular area. Dr. Zugiba explains that the ventricle wall is the section of the heart muscle that makes the heart beat. He notes that there has been recent injury, similar to situations where a person has been severely beaten in the chest area, as the heart muscle is inflamed.

Dr. Zugiba further explains that the white blood cells indicate inflammation and injury, adding that these can only exist if they are fed by a body that is living. He states that the flesh sample was alive at the moment it was collected. After hearing this, Mike Willesee pauses, realizing the apparent miracle; he needs a moment to regain his professional demeanor and compose himself. Dr. Zugiba confirms that if human tissue were placed in water, the white blood cells would dissolve within minutes and cease to exist.

Mike Willesee then reveals to Dr. Zugiba that the tissue sample had been stored in tap water for a month, followed by three years in distilled water, and Dr. Zugiba says that this is absolutely unbelievable, adding that no explanation can be given by science for such a phenomenon. Mike then reveals that this tissue came from a Eucharistic Host, and Dr. Zugiba says that this is outside the ability of science to explain.

Outside the ability of science to explain... Mike Willesee and Ron Tesoriero have filmed interviews with Dr. Zugiba, as well as other aspects of the miracle, and they have incorporated this footage into a documentary.

It has been speculated that there is a symbolic significance to the location of the flesh sample, the organ that it comes from. It comes from the left ventricle of the heart, which pumps blood to all parts of the body. Through the Eucharist, Jesus pumps life to all members of His Church.

Just as He spoke to Thomas two thousand years ago, Jesus is speaking to you and I now... *Do not be unbelieving, but believe.*

As you will see below, similar Eucharistic miracles have occurred in several other countries recently. You will find that these miracles tend be somewhat similar, but I provide them as additional physical evidence of Jesus' Real Presence in the Eucharist.

Sokolka, Poland, 2008[39]

It's October 12, 2008 in Sokolka, Poland. Parishioners are receiving Communion at the 8:30am Mass at Saint Anthony's Church. The celebrant, Father Filip Zdrodowski, accidentally drops the Eucharist. Following proper Church protocol, he places it into a small silver vessel containing water, the vessel often used by priests to wash

---

[39] Real Presence Eucharistic Education and Adoration Association, *The Eucharistic Miracles of the World,* 222-227.

their fingers after distributing Communion. He intends to dissolve the Host in the water. After the Mass, the sacristan, Sister Julia Dubowska, takes the silver vessel containing the Host, and for increased safety, pours it into another vessel. She then locks the vessel in the safe, where the chalices are kept.

A week later, on October 19, 2008, about 8am, Sister Dubowska opens the safe, finding the Host almost dissolved, but with unusual red clots in the center, and she immediately calls the priests. Although most of the Host has dissolved, there remains a very small piece of consecrated bread, tightly interconnected to the "strange red clot." The pastor contacts the Metropolitan Curia of Białystok. Archbishop Edward Ozorowski, together with the Chancellor of the Curia, priests and professors examine the Host and are astonished. They decide to wait and see what develops.

On October 29, 2008, the vessel containing the Host is taken to the parish chapel and locked inside the tabernacle. The next day, by order of Archbishop Gniedziejko, the partially dissolved Host is delicately removed with a small spoon and placed on a pure white corporal (cloth) with a red cross embroidered on its center. The corporal is kept in the case used for storing Hosts, and it is locked again in the tabernacle. The Host eventually "fuses" with the corporal, and the red "clot" dries.

In early January 2009, the Curia of Białystok contacts

two well-known specialists in anatomical pathological anatomy, Professor Maria Elżbieta Sobaniec-Łotowska and Professor Stanisław Sulkowski, both from the Medical University of Białystok, to scientifically analyze samples from the bloodstained Host. The professors independently analyze the samples, and Professor Sulkowski is unaware that the sample came from a Host. The professors use optical microscopes and transmission electronic microscopes, and both reach the same conclusion: the sample appears to be human cardiac muscle tissue and is still alive. In addition, the cardiac muscle tissue is experiencing the final phase that precedes death.

With this in mind, the Metropolitan Curia of Białystok releases a declaration concerning the Eucharistic Miracle of Sokółka. The declaration notes that on October 12, 2008, a consecrated Host fell during Holy Communion, and it was placed into a vessel containing water. The Host was later removed from the water and placed on a corporal (or sheet) inside the tabernacle. A sample of the Host, after being independently examined by two histopathology professors at the University of Medicine of Białystok, was declared to look like myocardial tissue. The declaration also notes that no intervention by a third party was found.

The professors notice that the Host sample, even after remaining in water and on the corporal for a long period of time, does not undergo self-destruction by the action of intracellular enzymes. Ordinarily, autolysis, or the breakdown of tissue by self-produced enzymes, occurs over time; however, no traces of this are found.

After some suggested that bacteria might have caused the red color, Professor Sulkowski observes that the substance found on the corporal did not change in appearance, even though it was not stabilized or preserved at a particular temperature. It did, in fact, dry, after being removed from the water. With this in mind, Professor Sulkowski notes that if bacteria caused the miracle, the material would have changed appearance, looking completely different after only a week.

Could someone have placed a fragment of human flesh into the tabernacle? This would be impossible, due to the tight interconnection between the fragments of the Host and the fibers of the human tissue. They penetrated each other, as if a fragment of bread suddenly transformed itself into human tissue. Professor Sobaniec-Łotowska, noting that this fact has been of particular importance for her, affirms that even NASA scientists, with the most modern scientific techniques, could not recreate this artificially!

Legnica, Poland, 2013[40]

[40] "Eucharistic Miracle of Legnica 1," Real Presence Eucharistic Education and Adoration Association, accessed August 11, 2020, http://therealpresence.org/eucharst/mir/english_pdf/Legnica1. pdf; "Eucharistic Miracle of Legnica 2," Real Presence Eucharistic Education and Adoration Association, accessed August 11, 2020,

During Christmas Mass, 2013, in Saint Hyacinth's Church in Legnica, a Host accidentally falls to the ground during the distribution of Holy Communion. Following Church protocol and Canon Law, the Host is immediately placed into a container filled with water and closed in the tabernacle. Several days later, on January 4, 2014, Father Andrzej Ziombra and several other priests check to see if the Host has dissolved. Instead, they notice that the Host has not dissolved, and that a red spot, covering a fifth of its surface, has appeared.

Stefan Cichy, then Bishop of Legnica, decides to establish a theological scientific commission to analyze the event. The Wroclaw Forensic Medicine Institute immediately determines that neither bacteria nor fungi caused the Host to turn red. A second histopathological analysis indicates that some fragments appear to be myocardial tissue. Human DNA is also found.

An additional opinion is then sought, without specifying the source of the samples, at the Institute of Forensic Medicine in Szczecin. The Institute of Forensic Medicine in Szczecin uses a different method of analysis. The results of the scientific analysis are presented to the Vatican's Congregation for the Doctrine of the Faith, and they recognize that the event was of a supernatural nature.

---

http://therealpresence.org/eucharst/mir/english_pdf/Legnica2.pdf.

Professor Barbara Engel, doctor and cardiologist, one of the scientists involved in the analysis, announces the following at a press conference: using UV rays with an orange filter, the material was analyzed and the results were unambiguous. They found myocardial fibers, characteristic of myocardial tissue with modifications that often appear during an agony.

On April 17, 2016, Monsignor Zbigniew Kiernikowskiego, the new Bishop of Legnica, following the instructions of the Holy See, announces during Mass that Father Andrzej Ziombra, the parish priest, should provide a location for exhibition of this precious relic and make it available for adoration by the faithful.

Tixtla, Mexico, 2006[41]

In this miracle, the Host actually "bleeds" during Mass. It's October 21, 2006 at Saint Martin of Tours parish in Tixtla, Mexico. The pastor of this church, Father Leopoldo Roque, has invited Father Raymundo Reyna Esteban to lead a retreat at his parish. Father Roque and another priest are distributing Communion, assisted by a religious sister. Suddenly, the sister turns to Father Roque with tears in her eyes. The Host that she has taken to give to a parishioner has begun to effuse a reddish substance ... it appears to be bleeding.

---

[41] Real Presence Eucharistic Education and Adoration Association, *The Eucharistic Miracles of the World,* 180-183.

The local Bishop, Alejo Zavala Castro, convenes a Theological Commission of Investigation. In October of 2009, he invites Dr. Ricardo Castañón Gómez to lead the scientific analysis of this event. The Mexican ecclesiastical authorities turn to Dr. Gomez because he assisted in the scientific analysis of the Eucharistic miracle in Buenos Aires at Saint Mary's earlier. Scientific research is conducted between October 2009 and October 2012. Several scientists, including Professor Carlos Parellada of the Franciso Marroquín University in Guatemala and Professor John Compagno, a preeminent histopathologist, are involved in this research. The Gene Ex genetics laboratory in Bolivia also participates in the study. The Gene Ex laboratory confirms that the blood is human, and the blood type is AB.

The research reveals some very unusual things about the Host sample. John Compagno discovers the presence of mesenchymal cells and tissue of white blood cells and red blood cells. An analysis of phyto-chemical markers confirms that it is live cardiac muscle. Normally, after forty-eight hours, tissue dies, but at the time of this discovery, three months had passed. This is unexplainable by modern science.

You might ask, could someone have placed human blood or human tissue onto the Host? The scientists considered this question. In 2010, using digital microscopic penetration, ultraviolet rays and intense white light, they discovered that tissue in the upper part of the Host showed some dry coagulated blood. Under the dry coagulated blood, however, there was also fresh blood. If someone had purposely placed blood onto the Host, it could never have remained fresh for this length of time (from 2006 to 2010) in the internal part of the Host. In addition, research concluded that blood flowed from the interior to the exterior of the Host. This would not have been the case, had someone added blood from the exterior.

In a pastoral letter, Alejo Zavala Castro, Bishop of the Diocese of Chilpancingo-Chilapa, announced his recognition of the Eucharistic miracle. He noted that this is a marvelous sign of God's love, confirming the real presence of Christ in the Eucharist. He added that as Bishop of the Diocese, he recognizes the supernatural character of the events related to the Bleeding Host of Tixtla, declaring this case to be a Divine Sign.

The results of the scientific research were presented at an international symposium, held by the Diocese of Chilpancingo, on May 25, 2013.

The results noted the following. The reddish substance appears to be blood, with hemoglobin and human DNA. Forensic experts in two studies using different methodologies have found that the substance comes from the interior, discrediting the theory that someone could have placed it onto the Host from the exterior. The blood type found is type AB, similar to the blood type found on the Shroud of Turin and in the Host from the Miracle of Lanciano. Intact white blood cells and red blood cells were found. The tissue corresponds to the muscle of the heart. Following the scientific results and the conclusions presented by the theological committee, the Bishop of Chilpancingo, his Eminence Alejo Zavala Castro, announced that this event does not have a natural explanation and is not subject to manipulation of the enemy.

Lanciano, Italy, 750 / Scientifically Analyzed 1970[42]

I chose to cover this miracle from over twelve centuries ago because it was the subject of an in-depth scientific analysis in 1970. An unnamed monastic priest from the Order of Saint Basil was celebrating Mass in the Church of Saint Francis in the year 750. This priest doubted the real presence of Jesus in the Eucharist. After speaking the words of the consecration, the Host suddenly changed into a circle of flesh and the wine was transformed into visible blood. The congregation rushed to the altar, and, marveling at the sight, spread the news to other townspeople. The flesh remained intact, but the blood in the chalice soon divided into five pellets of equal size. The flesh is still intact today.

---

[42] Real Presence Eucharistic Education and Adoration Association, *The Eucharistic Miracles of the World, 132-135; Joan Carroll Cruz, Eucharistic Miracles and Eucharistic Phenomena in the Lives of the Saints* (Charlotte: TAN Books, 1991), 3, 5-7.

In 1970, the Archbishop of Lanciano and the Provincial Superior of the Conventual Franciscans at Abruzzo, with Rome's approval, asked Dr. Edward Linoli to perform a thorough scientific examination of the relics of this miracle. Dr. Linoli, then director of the hospital of Arezzo and professor of anatomy, histology, chemistry, and clinical microscopy, presented a detailed report on March 4, 1971 describing the various studies that he carried out. The basic results are listed here:

The tissue sample is truly flesh, specifically muscular striated tissue of the myocardium. The blood is true blood, tested with a chromatographic analysis, which indicates this fact as indisputable. The immunological study shows with absolute certainty that the flesh and blood are human. The immuno-hematological test shows with absolute certainty that both are of the blood type AB, the same blood type found on the Shroud of Turin. No traces of salt infiltrations or preservative substances used in antiquity for embalming were found.

Professor Linoli also availed himself of the services of Dr. Ruggero Bertelli, professor emeritus of normal human anatomy at the University of Siena. Dr. Bertelli concurred with all of Professor Linoli's conclusions, and he presented an official document to this effect.

The blood type AB has been found in other Eucharistic miracles. The reference to the Shroud is particularly interesting, as blood type AB was also found on the

Shroud of Turin. Professor Linoli discarded the hypothesis of a hoax carried out in past centuries. This report was published in *The Sclavo Notebooks in Diagnostics* (Collection #3, 1971).

Considering the question of a possible fraud, Professor Linoli noted that the blood, had it been taken from a cadaver, would have altered rapidly through decay and spoilage. He also believed that only a hand experienced in anatomic dissection could extract such an expert cut from a hollow internal organ such as the heart, a cut made tangentially, a round cut, thick on the outer edges and lessening gradually and uniformly into nothingness in the central area.

Professor Linoli's findings generated great interest in the scientific world, and in 1973, the chief Advisory Board of the World Health Organization appointed a scientific commission to corroborate his findings. The scientific commission's work lasted fifteen months and included some five hundred tests. Their reply fully corroborated Professor Linoli's conclusions.

The commission found that the fragments taken from Lanciano could in no way be likened to embalmed tissue. The commission declared the fragments to be living tissue because they responded rapidly to the clinical reactions distinctive of humans. An extract, summarizing the work of the Medical Commission of the UN, published in December 1976 in New York and Geneva, stated that science, aware of its limits, has come to a halt, and it is unable to provide an explanation for this.

Science, aware of its limits, has come to a halt in attempting to explain this miracle.

Even if someone were to claim that all of these miracles were frauds, which would be very difficult to support, given the amount of scientific documentation, it would still be necessary to explain where the tissue samples came from. As noted above, the tissue samples themselves are miraculous, for the reasons discussed above.

Personal Relationship – Spending Time with People We Love

Jesus performed these miracles because He wants you to believe in His Real Presence in the Eucharist. Personal relationships include physical presence; we spend time with people we love. Jesus wants to make it clear that He is present within the Eucharist, so that you will visit Him in Person. He waits for you in the tabernacle. He wants to spend time with you, and He wants you to come and converse with Him. You may not hear Him speak audibly, but He will communicate with you regardless. He wants you to come and tell Him personally about your fears, difficulties and problems; He wants to hear of your joys, plans and whatever is going on with you. He also wants you to receive Him in Holy Communion (after going to

Confession if you have any mortal sins to confess).

He repeats His words to Saint Thomas in the Gospel: *Do not persist in your unbelief, but believe.*

EXAMPLE #3: Scientifically Analyzed Tilma from the Apparitions of Our Lady of Guadalupe[43]

Next, I discuss the ongoing miracle of Juan Diego's tilma (jacket) from the apparitions of Our Lady of Guadalupe. The tilma has been through many scientific analyses. Science is unable to explain it. I describe this as an "ongoing" miracle because the tilma should have fallen apart after twenty years, since it is made of plant fiber. However, the tilma has lasted for more than four and a half centuries. The tilma is a beautiful artifact full of mystery. Many books have been written about it, and many scientists have studied it. How was it created?

To summarize, the Blessed Mother asked Juan Diego, a poor Mexican, to tell the bishop that she wanted a special church or chapel built. The bishop asked for evidence. Juan Diego brought him beautiful Castilian roses, which could never have bloomed in that particular climate at that time of year. As he displayed these to the bishop, an amazing picture appeared on the back of his tilma (jacket), a beautiful and mysterious image, full of unusual facts and hidden secrets. This image greatly strengthened the faith of the people of Mexico. It has also strengthened the faith of the entire world. The enduring properties of this

---

[43] Francis Johnston, *The Wonder of Guadalupe* (Charlotte: TAN Books, 1981), 124-148. "Our Lady's image on the Tilma," Our Lady of Guadalupe, accessed December 23, 2021, https://olg.cc/about/about-our-patroness/our-ladys-image-on-the-tilma/.

sacred image have caused many to recognize its supernatural quality. In 1976, an agnostic architect named Ramirez Vasquez asked permission to study the image, and after completing his studies, he became a Catholic. (Artist's rendition of the image from Our Lady of Guadalupe: https://www.cathopic.com/photo/1983-mi-morenita. Used with permission.)

Juan Diego's Tilma: Science's Verdict

The tilma has been through a number of scientific investigations, and science is unable to explain it ... how it remains to this day, how its colors were applied, why its colors have not faded, and a number of other things about it. Before I cover these, however, I want to note another interesting fact. The tilma survived a deliberate attempt to destroy it.

Under the rule of Plutarco Calles, during the persecution of the Church in Mexico in the 1920's, a time bomb was placed beneath the tilma. It was a calculated effort to discourage the faith of the Mexican people. On November 14, 1921, a powerful bomb was hidden in a vase of flowers immediately beneath the sacred image. At 10:30am, during Mass, the bomb exploded with shattering force, ripping marble and masonry and twisting a heavy iron cross. Somehow, however, no one in the congregation was seriously injured. Perhaps even more astonishing, the sacred image was entirely unscathed. Not even the thin protective glass covering it was affected. The twisted iron cross was later placed on display to remind pilgrims of the miraculous protection given the sacred image on that fateful day. A special Chapel of Reparation to the Blessed Sacrament was created to atone for crimes committed during the Calles regime. Ironically, the blast only strengthened the faith of the people of Mexico, increasing their devotion to Jesus in the Blessed Sacrament and reinforcing their confidence in Mary's intercession.

In another incident, the sacred image was almost destroyed by a careless workman. In 1791, while cleaning the image's gold and silver frame, a workman accidentally spilled nitric acid on it. Rather than destroying the delicate plant fabric, the acid left a barely discernible watermark on the image.

Professor Philip Callahan, a biophysicist at the University of Florida, studied the sacred image in 1979, and he noted a number of findings. Professor Callahan studied the environment in which the image had been placed. Callahan measured over six hundred thousand microwatts of near ultraviolet light emanating from a single votive candle. If you multiply this by the thousands of candles that have been used over the centuries around the image, it's remarkable that the colors have not faded. Callahan noted that most color pigments, whether organic or inorganic, quickly fade when exposed to excess ultraviolet light; blues are especially susceptible to this.

Additionally, the image has been handled by countless pilgrims during its existence. Pilgrims have touched, kissed, felt and held the image. Some of the over-zealous have discretely removed threads from the image, keeping them as relics. In 1753, Miguel Cabrera counted that the tilma was touched over five hundred times during a two-hour period. Despite all of this, the image remains well preserved.

Picture above shows an artist's representation of the image of Our Lady of Guadalupe. Image by Marcaroni from Pixabay https://pixabay.com/illustrations/our-lady-of-guadalupe-4542832/

The Tilma Studied with Infrared Photography

In May 1979, two high-ranking American scientists, Professor Philip Callahan (noted above) and Professor Jody Smith of Pensacola, Florida took approximately sixty photographs of the sacred image. Callahan and Smith used infrared radiation for many of these photographs in an effort to find an artist's drawing underneath the image. At the outset, Professor Smith noted that she had an interest in doing what William James suggested a hundred years ago, to bring science and religion together. She added that in our culture today, we often live lives that are too compartmentalized. Infrared photography is able to unmask overpainting and alterations, and it has become a common tool in art research. In a subsequent report, Callahan said that one cannot consider the study of an art piece to be complete without using infrared photography; a valid scientific study is incomplete without this.

On May 7, 1979, in the presence of a bishop, a policeman and a number of workmen, the tests were conducted on the tilma itself. The results of the investigation are summarized as follows. Science cannot explain the image, including how the color was rendered or how the brightness of the image has been preserved over the centuries. There is definitely no protective varnish, under-drawing or sizing present. The tilma should have rotted long ago, since it does not have sizing. Without protective varnishing, candlelight, smoke and other pollutants should have ruined the image. High magnification does not reveal any detectable signs of fading or cracking, which cannot be explained after four hundred and fifty years. Somehow, the coarse weave of the tilma has been intentionally used, with precision, to add depth to the face on the image.

Callahan noted that, although it might seem unusual for a scientist to say this, he believes that the original picture is miraculous. The infrared close-up pictures show no brush marks. Callahan believes that no painter could have used a tilma, with all of its weave imperfections, to accentuate the shadows and highlights and convey such realism. Callahan noted that studying the image has moved him, more than anything else in his life. As he approached the image, getting very close to it, Callahan explains, he had the same feeling that others must have felt while studying the Shroud of Turin. He added that he believes in logical explanations up to a certain point, but life has no logical explanation. Callahan noted that after you break something down into atoms, according to Einstein, at least, what comes next is God.

If the image is not a painting, what is it? What is producing its color? Richard Kuhn, director of the chemistry department at the Kaiser Wilhelm Institute in Heidelberg, and German Nobel Prize Winner in chemistry, investigated. In 1936, he was given two fibers from the sacred image, one red and one yellow. He examined the fibers and made a startling announcement. There was no coloring of any kind used in the fibers. The material used to produce the color was unknown to science, being neither animal, nor vegetable nor mineral dyes. Synthetic coloring was ruled out, since that was developed three centuries after the creation of the image.

Reflections of People Within the Eye of the Image

On May 29, 1951, a draughtsman named J. Carlos Salinas Chavez was using a powerful magnifying glass while examining a photograph of the face on the image. As he looked at the pupil of the right eye, he made an astonishing discovery. There within the pupil was the bust of a bearded man. The archbishop of Mexico City, Luis Marie Martinez, set up a special committee to investigate this. On December 11, 1955, the discovery was made public, together with the fact that the human face in the eye of the image had been positively identified from a contemporary painting. It was the face of Juan Diego!

This was further studied by two oculists; Drs. Javier Torroello Buene and Rafael Torifa Lavoignet examined the eyes of the image. On July 23, 1956, Dr. Lavoignet conducted a meticulous examination of the eyes using an ophthalmoscope (an instrument used to inspect the retina and other parts of the eye). He noted the following. A human bust is visible within the cornea of the eyes, and the distortion and location of the image are identical with what one would expect to find in a normal human eye. By directing the light of the ophthalmoscope onto the pupil of a human eye, you can see a reflection of light shining on its outer circle. By changing the lenses of the ophthalmoscope and following this reflection, you can obtain the image at the back of the eye. When directing the light of the ophthalmoscope onto the Blessed Virgin's eye, the same light reflection is seen ... the pupil lights up in a diffused way, providing the impression of hollow relief. It is impossible to obtain this reflection on a flat surface, and moreover, one that is as opaque as this picture. No other paintings provided this reflection in the eyes of their subjects, but the eyes of the Virgin Mary in the image give the impression of life.

The eyes of the Virgin Mary of Guadalupe give the impression of life. Could an artist achieve such a feat today, working on the coarse canvas of a Mexican tilma? Remember, this image was produced over four and a half centuries ago. If Juan Diego's tilma had been color film, and if it had photographed the Virgin Mary (although she was invisible) at the very moment the sacred image appeared, it could have captured the reflection of Juan Diego in her eyes. This was an incredible fact that remained hidden for four hundred years, only to be discovered in our time by modern science. This is another example of faith and science complementing one another, working together to explain a mystery.

Aztec Interpretation of the Image

The sacred image conveyed messages that would be immediately understood by an Aztec audience in 1531. The Aztecs were very familiar with reading pictographs. By standing in front of the sun, the Lady communicated that she was greater than Huitzilopochtli, the terrifying Aztec sun-god. Her foot rested on a crescent moon, which signified their principal deity, the serpent-god

Quetzalcoatl, whom she had plainly vanquished. She wore a mantle of blue-green hue, the color worn by Aztec royalty, indicating that she was a Queen. The stars distributed across her mantle communicated that she was greater than the stars of heaven, which the Aztecs worshiped as gods. However, her hands were joined in prayer and her head was bowed in reverence, indicating that she could not be God. The black cross presented on the gold brooch at her neck indicated that her religion was that of the Spaniards, who used the same cross.

Star Constellations on the Tilma[44]

There is much more to the tilma, such as constellations of stars found within the mantle, constellations that corresponded precisely with the constellations visible in Mexico City on the morning of December 12, 1531. There are also various meanings attributed to these constellations and where they appear on the image in relation to the Lady.

Mary Reaching Out to You As Your Mother

When Jesus saw his mother and the disciple there whom he loved, he said to his mother, "Woman, behold, your son." Then he said to the disciple, "Behold, your mother." And from that hour the disciple took her into his home. (John 19:26-27)

[44] Robert A. Sungenis, "New Discoveries of the Constellations on the Tilma of Our Lady of Guadalupe," *Catholic Apologetics International* (2007), 2-3.

Why would Mary appear on Juan Diego's tilma? Why would she visit us in the apparitions of Our Lady of Guadalupe? She did this because she wants you to know that she is your mother. In the passage quoted above, Jesus, in His hour of extreme agony upon the Cross, entrusts Mary to His disciple John as his Mother. Here, John represents all of mankind; Jesus is entrusting His Mother to all of us. As His suffering reaches its climax, Jesus thinks of us, and He bestows the benefit of Mary's maternal care upon us. Mary hears Jesus telling her, "Woman, behold your son," and she takes these words very seriously. As the mother of the King of Kings, she is a Queen, and quite a powerful one. This powerful Queen wants you to have a relationship with her and to call upon her as your own mother. Jesus has enjoyed the maternal care of Mary, and He wants you to enjoy the benefits of her maternal care as well. Like us, she is only a creature, but she has an unbelievable amount of influence over her Son, and He is very responsive to her requests.

During one of Mary's apparitions at Guadalupe, she spoke the following words to Juan Diego:[45]

Know and understand well, you my most humble son, that I am the ever-virgin Holy Mary, Mother of the True God for whom we live, of the Creator of all things, Lord of heaven and

---

[45] "'I am your mother': Our Lady of Guadalupe," Society of Saint Pius X, December 11, 2014, accessed October 24, 2021, https://sspx.org/en/i-am-your-mother-lady-of-guadalupe.

the earth. I wish that a temple be erected here quickly, so I may therein exhibit and give all my love, compassion, help, and protection, because I am your merciful mother, to you, and to all the inhabitants on this land and all the rest who love me, invoke and confide in me; listen there to their lamentations, and remedy all their miseries, afflictions and sorrows.

Mary wants to have a personal relationship with you as your mother. What is her goal in this relationship? Her goal is always to bring you to her Son, Jesus. She is quite good at doing this, and saints tell us that the fastest way to Jesus is through Mary. Mary will always tell her children what she told the servers at the wedding feast in Cana in the Gospel of John. Mary, referring to her Son, Jesus, says: *Do whatever he tells you.* (John 2:5)

Spiritual Lightsaber

The rosary is the scourge of the devil.
—Pope Adrian VI

The rosary is the weapon that wins all battles.
—Padre Pio

The soul which recommends itself to me by the recitation of the Rosary, shall not perish. —
Blessed Virgin Mary

I provide multiple quotes because this is a very important prayer, and many have commented on its importance. At Fatima, the Blessed Mother specifically asked that we pray the rosary every day. I myself must practice what I preach. I pray my rosary during the day or in the evening. I wield my Lightsaber every day. My goal in this book is to show you why you will want to be wielding yours as well.

Where does this Lightsaber analogy come from? As noted, Padre Pio repeatedly called the rosary a weapon: *The rosary, that is my weapon.* Again, *The rosary is the weapon that wins all battles.*[46] Even a pope, Blessed Pope Pius IX, engaged in this sort of language: *Give me an army saying the Rosary and I will conquer the world.*[47] While reading the stories that follow, you will discover that the Rosary is a spiritual Lightsaber, a strong weapon against evil and a powerful means of calling down God's blessings. I credit Father Donald Calloway, MIC, for the analogy of the Lightsaber.[48] The analogy is very fitting. In this book, you will see just how fitting.

---

[46] Michael Ogunu, "The Rosary: A Weapon to Win All Battles," *The Southern Cross*, October 31, 2017, accessed November 14, 2021, https://www.scross.co.za/2017/10/the-rosary-a-weapon-to-win-all-battles/.

[47] "Best 19 Quotes on the Rosary," TFP Student Action, accessed October 17, 2021, https://tfpstudentaction.org/get-involved/campus-rosary-crusade/quotes-on-the-rosary.

[48] Donald H. Calloway, MIC. *10 Wonders of the Rosary* (Stockbridge, MA: Marian Press, 2019), 23.

I wrote this book because most people do not appreciate the true power of the Rosary; even people familiar with the Rosary do not understand the true extent of its power. What makes the Rosary powerful?

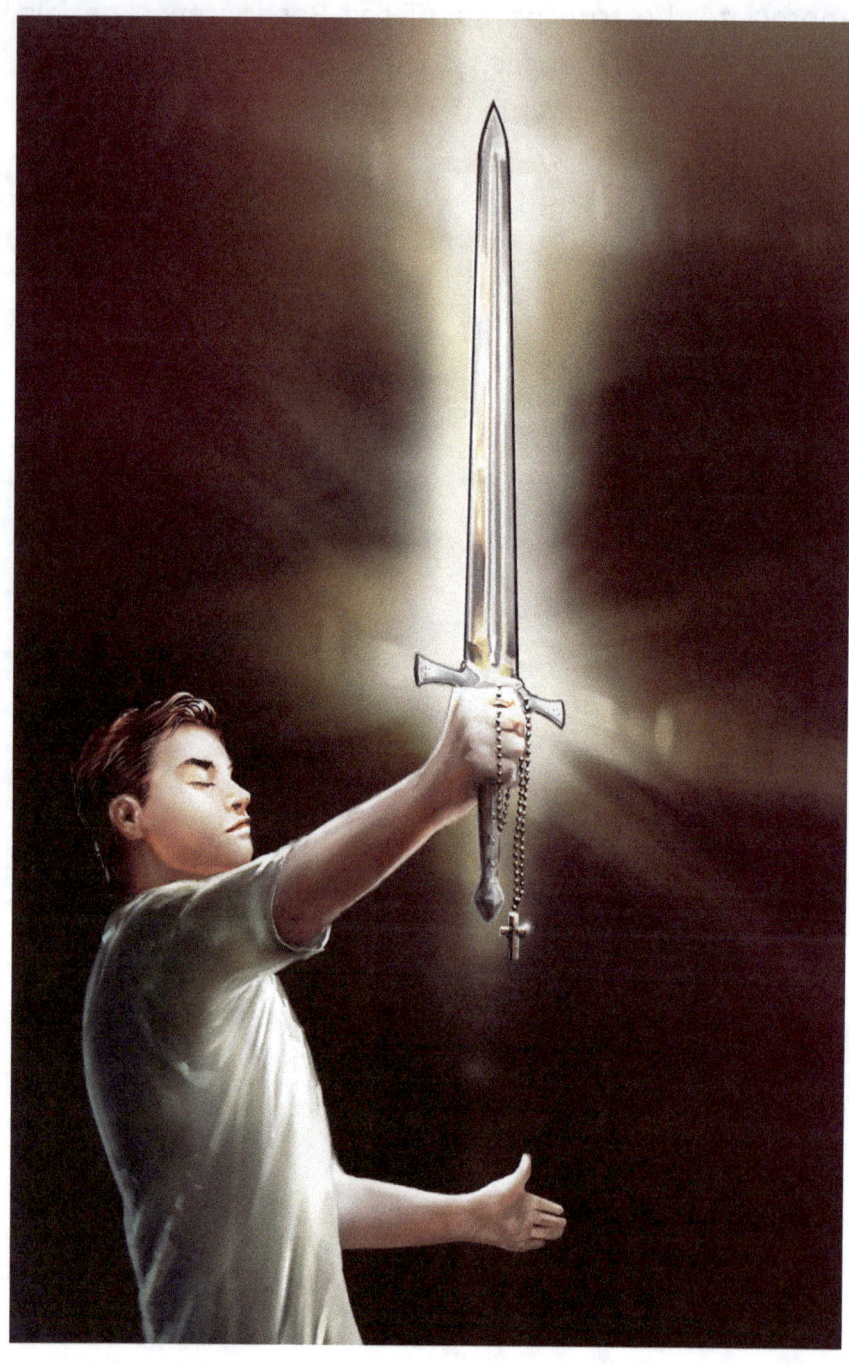

WHY WOULD A SPIRITUAL LIGHTSABER BE POWERFUL?

In the second chapter of John's Gospel, we find a clue. Here, we read about a newly married couple running out of wine at a wedding celebration in Cana. As you might guess, this would be an embarrassing and awkward moment for a couple. Things looked rather hopeless, until ... Mary became involved. I don't know this for a fact, but I strongly believe that Mary decided to take action entirely on her own initiative. She quickly tells Jesus what He already knew, *They have no wine.* (John 2:3) Mary asks Jesus to perform His first public miracle to solve the problem. As miracles go, this seems like a rather insignificant need. Don't get me wrong. Wine at a wedding is important, but no one is dying; no one has been seriously injured. No one needs to be cured. It seems like an unlikely place for Jesus' first public miracle. Yet, Mary intercedes for the couple, and Jesus responds. Jesus performs a miracle, producing very good wine, and lots of it. *You have kept the good wine until now.* (John 2:10) As a good Son, Jesus wants to honor His Mother, and He accommodates the request. Mary specifically says in Luke 1:49, *The Mighty One has done great things for me, and holy is his name.* Jesus continues to do great things for Mary, just as He did at the wedding feast in Cana.

There is another reason why the rosary is powerful. Mary is often pictured holding the baby Jesus while trampling the serpent beneath her feet. The serpent is of course Satan, as he appeared in the Garden of Eden when our story first began (Genesis 3:1). The picture of Mary crushing the serpent's head is a direct reference to the great prophecy made by God Himself in Genesis 3:15:[49]

To paraphrase, God states that the woman will crush Satan's head while he will wait to attack her heel.

The Fathers of the Church have taught that Mary is the woman mentioned here, the "Woman of Genesis."[50] Jesus wants to honor His mother by granting her the privilege of crushing Satan's head. Satan, being incredibly proud, is all the more humiliated when he is overcome by a mere creature, by a humble woman. One way that Mary overcomes Satan is through the prayer that specifically honors her, the Rosary.

---

[49] Here I paraphrase the Douay-Rheims Bible version. Some versions of the Bible replace "she" with "he" when saying *"she shall crush thy head..."* This question is considered at length in: Fra. Gabriel M. Mesina, "Christ and Mary revealed in Genesis 3:15," *Missio Immaculatae Magazine*, May 24, 2017. Mary of course cannot crush Satan's head **without Jesus' help and grace,** since Mary is only a creature.

[50] Pius IX, *Ineffabilis* Deus, apostolic constitution, Papal Encyclicals Online, December 8, 1854, accessed November 14, 2021, https://www.papalencyclicals.net/pius09/p9ineff.htm.

In summary, the Rosary is powerful for many reasons, but I will focus on three. First, Jesus wants to honor His mother. The Rosary honors Mary by repeating the greeting made to her by the Angel Gabriel (Luke 1:28) and Elizabeth (Luke 1:42) in the Hail Mary. Second, as Jesus' mother, Mary has a ton of influence over Him. In praying the Rosary, we harness the power of Mary's influence, asking her to intercede with her Son on our behalf. Third, Jesus has granted Mary a special role in the effort to crush Satan's head.

Since the Rosary is a powerful prayer, we would expect to find saints and holy people using it. Most of us have heard of Mother Teresa, the saint who ministered to the poorest of the poor in India. She was a strong advocate of the Rosary, asking people to pray it every day. Another famous saint is Padre Pio. Padre Pio died in 1968, and he bore the stigmata, the visible wounds of Christ. As you will learn, Padre Pio prayed countless Rosaries, and he was rarely seen without a Rosary in his hand.

WHO IS PADRE PIO?

Padre Pio, the saint I quoted in the title of this book, is difficult to summarize, as his influence spans the globe; countless books, articles and videos have been created about him. How did a humble Italian priest living in Italy during the Second World War dramatically affect the lives of so many people across the world? Heroic holiness, a great sense of humor, and unbelievable spiritual gifts … all of these made him irresistible to pilgrims who sought him out on every occasion. Primarily known for the stigmata, the bleeding wounds of Christ, Padre Pio suffered from pain in his hands, feet and side[51] for over fifty years.[52] In addition to the stigmata, he possessed the gifts of prophecy, healing and the "odor of sanctity," a beautiful fragrance which often accompanied him and/or indicated his intercession. Padre Pio was the first priest in the history of the Church to receive the stigmata.[53]

Padre Pio was especially known for his sense of

[51] Diane Allen, *Pray, Hope, and Don't Worry: True Stories of Padre Pio Book I* (Padre Pio Press, 2012), 6.
[52] Allen, *Pray, Hope, and Don't Worry: True Stories of Padre Pio Book I*, 394.
[53] Allen, *Pray, Hope, and Don't Worry: True Stories of Padre Pio Book I*, 116.

humor, and he always loved a good joke. Even as a child, he thoroughly enjoyed teasing his sisters. With delight he would sneak up behind his sister, Felicita, as she washed herself in the bathtub, and he would dunk her head into the soapy water.[54] "Franci," as he was called, often enjoyed pranks as well. One day, Mercurio Scocca, a playmate, buried him under a pile of corn shocks as he slept underneath a tree during siesta time. When he awoke, Franci found himself in darkness, and he screamed for his mother as the boys thundered with laughter. The next day, Franci found an opportunity to play a prank on Mercurio; he saw Mercurio taking a siesta on a small farm wagon. Seeing the opportunity, Franci quietly rolled the wagon to the top of a nearby hill. He then pushed the wagon down the hill, and Mercurio awakened to quite a ride. Fortunately, the wagon was caught by a tree without any problems.

Franci's love of pranks continued into his late teens as he prepared for the priesthood.[55] One night, Franci's community was praying at midnight, and he spied a young novice who was rather nervous and "afraid of his own shadow." After returning from the bathroom, Franci happened to be carrying a towel. Spying a table with two candles and a human skull sitting upon it, Franci snuck up behind the table and waited for the young novice to

---

[54] Patricia Treece, Meet *Padre Pio: Beloved Mystic, Miracle Worker and Spiritual Guide* (Cincinnati: Charis, 2001), 7.
[55] Treece, *Meet Padre Pio: Beloved Mystic, Miracle Worker and Spiritual Guide*, 15.

pass by. (Novices would sometimes meditate on a human skull, representing life's brevity.) As the novice walked by, Franci groaned, flapping his towel at him, and the novice ran away, terrified! Franci tried to calm him down, chasing after him, but the novice only screamed louder! In his later years as a priest, Padre Pio felt no remorse for his prank. In fact, he loved to tell the story for the rest of his life! Great holiness does not mean that you can't have fun, and Padre Pio exemplifies this fact very well.

Pope Paul VI summarized the life of Padre Pio in the following words: *What fame he had. How many followers from around the world. Why? Was it because he was a philosopher, a scholar, or because he had means at his disposal? No, it was because he said Mass humbly, heard confessions from morning until night and was a marked representative of the stigmata of Our Lord. He was truly a man of prayer and suffering.*[56]

Padre Pio's remarkable holiness did not in any way diminish his normality; he was incredibly normal. He was nothing like the "sour-faced saint," walking through life staring at the ground with a scowl on his face. Padre Pio spent time joking and conversing with friends, and he greatly enjoyed his 5:30pm beer, which he consumed every day at social time.[57] He especially liked American

---

[56] "A Short Biography," Padre Pio Devotions, accessed August 8, 2021, https://padrepiodevotions.org/a-short-biography/.
[57] Allen, *Pray, Hope, and Don't Worry: True Stories of Padre Pio Book I,* 253.

beer, and he would say that it was much better than the vegetable soup that he often ate at mid-day.[58] Granted, nearly everyone drank beer and wine as the water in Pietrelcina wasn't safe; nevertheless, Padre Pio was happy to partake. He looked forward to social time, and despite the suffering that he endured from the stigmata, he was jovial and told stories to visiting pilgrims and fellow religious.

---

[58] Allen, *Pray, Hope, and Don't Worry: True Stories of Padre Pio Book I,* 175.

PADRE PIO, TORCH BEARER OF THE ROSARY[59]

Padre Pio was rarely seen without a Rosary in his hands. By word and example, Padre Pio had much to say about this prayer, which he called *the weapon*. I must confess that Padre Pio's words and example have had a profound effect on me; they are one of the main reasons that I pray the Rosary every day.

Just before he died, while preparing for bed one evening, Padre Pio called out forcefully to his fellow friars to get him his "weapon." His friars, confused, wondered where this weapon might be. Padre Pio explained that it was inside his habit. Looking through the habit, the friars were once again confused, saying that they were unable to find any weapon; they could only find Rosary beads. Padre Pio then asked, *isn't the Rosary a weapon, isn't the Rosary truly a weapon?*

---

[59] "Padre Pio: Rosary Promoter," The Marian Room, July 21, 2021, accessed December 7, 2021, https://www.themarianroom.com/padre-pio-rosary-promoter/.

Padre Pio often referred to the Rosary this way; he looked upon the Rosary as one of his greatest means to bring people to God. As he explained on many occasions, to obtain defense and salvation, the Rosary is the weapon. He said that Mary has given us the weapon of the Rosary to fight against the tricks of the devil. He also explained that at Lourdes and Fatima, Mary recommended the Rosary because of its extraordinary usefulness for us and our time period. He added that we should take every opportunity to pray the Rosary, and basically pray it as much as we possibly can; after we have completed our duties, he said we should pray the Rosary with all the free time at our disposal. One day, Padre Pio picked up his Rosary, explaining to one of his visitors that with this weapon, one will be victorious in the battles!

After hearing such statements, I was tempted to ask, is Padre Pio taking the Rosary devotion a bit too far? Is Padre Pio exaggerating the power of the Rosary? Where do we see the power of the Rosary today?

THE ROSARY AND
BOKO HARAM[60]

It might sound like a bit of pious exaggeration to compare the Rosary to a Lightsaber. However, consider the case of Boko Haram in Nigeria. Many of you will remember April of 2014, when Boko Haram kidnapped a group of two hundred young girls from a school in Nigeria. The world held its breath, waiting to see what would happen next. Boko Haram is a radical Muslim group that decapitates non-Muslims, sometimes even burning them alive.

Bishop Oliver Dashe Doeme of the diocese of Maiduguri, Nigeria was praying his Rosary one evening when Jesus appeared to him, holding a sword. As Bishop Doeme looked on in amazement, Jesus extended the sword towards him. As he reached out to take it from Jesus, it changed into... a Rosary! As Bishop Doeme held the sword-become-rosary, Jesus repeated to him, "Boko Haram is gone! Boko Haram is gone! Boko Haram is gone!"

---

[60] Calloway, *10 Wonders of the Rosary*, 109-110.

Moved by the vision, Bishop Doeme began to actively promote the Rosary in his diocese. Bishop Doeme said it was clear from the vision that, with the Rosary, they would be able to expel Boko Haram. Several groups of girls were released on October 13, 2016. In May 2017, another eighty-three girls were released. Finally, on July 3, 2017, seven hundred Boko Haram members surrendered their weapons and turned themselves in to the Nigerian authorities. Here we see a horrible situation, overcome by the power of the Rosary. You can see Bishop Doeme on YouTube personally recounting his story.

In Nigeria, the Rosary took out a group of bad guys. How well does the Rosary stand up to a single villain, in a one-on-one attack?

THE ROSARY AND A
SERIAL KILLER[61]

During the late 1970's, the United States was victimized by the famous serial killer Ted Bundy. Bundy was notorious for raping and killing young women, and he was rather successful at it, brutally murdering at least thirty people during his reign of terror. His murders were often grisly, and he evaded capture for some time.

On January 15, 1978, Bundy broke into a sorority house at Florida State University in Tallahassee, Florida. He brutally assaulted and murdered several young women. He then came to the room of another young woman. Bundy slowly approached the door, moving stealthily. Gradually, he moved closer. He turned the knob ever so slightly and opened it, carefully glancing inside. What would happen next? Surely, Bundy wouldn't show mercy. Surely, he would chalk up his next victim. Suddenly, in a moment, the unthinkable happened! Bundy dropped his weapon and ran away! The young woman remained untouched. How could this be?

Police were called to the scene, and they found the

---

[61] Calloway, *10 Wonders of the Rosary*, 43-45.

young woman all right, but badly shaken. She was unwilling to speak to anyone but a priest. Monsignor William Kerr, who happened to be nearby, arrived and spoke with her. She told him that the killer had murdered two of her sorority sisters and severely harmed two others. When the killer came to her room, he opened the door, ready to kill her. As he saw her lying in bed ... he ran away.

Why would Bundy run? Why would he hesitate? What would cause him to abruptly flee? Bundy, of all people, was not faint of heart; he wasn't shy about attacking his victims. It seemed to defy explanation.

The young woman provided the answer to Monsignor Kerr. Before leaving for college, she had promised her mother that she would pray the Rosary every night for protection. True to her promise, she was praying the Rosary the night of Bundy's attack. When Bundy opened the door, he found her lying in bed asleep; she had fallen asleep that night praying the Rosary, and as she lay in bed, she held the Rosary in her hand.

Amazingly, when Ted Bundy was later on death row, he requested spiritual guidance from Monsignor Kerr, the very same priest who had spoken to the young woman. Bundy confided to Monsignor Kerr that he had no idea why he had not killed the young woman that night; he had every intention of doing so. When he reached her room, he said that a mysterious force prevented him from entering, and so he dropped his weapon ... and fled!

THE ROSARY AND A MAN TRAPPED IN THE WORLD TRADE CENTER ON 9/11[62]

Jedi have been known to pull out their Lightsaber in perilous situations, even if no one is personally attacking them. We find this scenario in the following story. John was trapped in the World Trade Center on 9/11. John believes that without the Blessed Mother's protection and the power of the Rosary, he would have died, as so many others did that day.

Born and raised in Manhattan, John had worked his whole life to be a successful investment agent, controlling millions of dollars for the company that he worked for. At age thirty-two, John was no longer a practicing Catholic, and despite his great career success, he felt unhappy. His parents were devout Catholics, but he had fallen away from the faith years before.

In the summer of 2001, several months before 9/11, a friend invited John to pray the Rosary with a prayer

[62] *"Rosary saves 9-11 survivor,"* America Needs Fatima, October 17, 2018, video, accessed November 14, 2021, https://youtu.be/Jkc_kpwiWQQ.

group. It was a special occasion, since a Fatima Pilgrim Virgin statue of the Blessed Mother would be there. John was going through a difficult period at the time, and remembering the comfort that family prayer had provided him in his youth, he agreed to attend. During the visit, a representative from America Needs Fatima, Jose Ferraz, offered him a Rosary. John kept the Rosary, occasionally praying it on his way to work.

John distinctly recalls that on the morning of 9/11, he left home without his Rosary. After walking three blocks, he realized it was missing, and feeling compelled to go back, he went home to retrieve it.

At 8:46am, American Airlines Flight 11 crashed into the North Tower of the World Trade Center, setting it ablaze with fire, death and destruction. As John's co-workers watched in horror, the plane exploded, sending dark plumes of smoke and ash into the morning sky, and the upper floors quickly began to disintegrate. John rushed to the elevator, only to find it stuck. With the stairs as his only option, he quickly descended, eventually finding a locked fire door. As John stood facing the door, he could hear fire raging all around him. Surrounded by death and despair, chaos and destruction, he remembers feeling a strange sense of calm. Why would he feel calm at this particular moment? Above him, flames burned out of control, and in front of him, a bolted door blocked any hope of escape. He was trapped, with precious seconds slipping away.

How long would he be able to breathe? How long before the floors above him would collapse? His options were gone. Everything looked hopeless. In desperation, he turned to prayer. He pulled out his Rosary, kneeling before the locked fire door. John once again felt a strange sense of calm. To this day, he can't explain why.

After several minutes of praying, the firemen arrived, breaking the lock and opening the doors. Despite all odds, despite fire and destruction, despite the maliciousness of radical Islamic terrorists, John ran down the stairs and out the door, to freedom.

In the days that followed, he couldn't help but ask, "Why me?!" After so many deaths that day, why did he survive? He concluded that only supernatural help, the help offered by Jesus through Mary to those who pray the Rosary, could have saved him.

DEFEATING THE GIANT GOLIATH

Many years ago, a young teenage boy, not much older than fifteen, took down a mighty Giant with a slingshot and a few small stones. 1 Samuel 17 tells the amazing story. It is not only edifying, but it also provides an image of the power of the Rosary. The ancient Israelites were taunted by a mighty warrior, Goliath of Gath, "six cubits and a span tall," which equates to about nine foot nine or almost ten feet tall! He was a formidable sight to behold, skilled in battle and larger than life. He walked in front of the Israelite soldiers, taunting them day after day.

...I defy the ranks of Israel today. Give me a man and let us fight together. When Saul and all Israel heard this challenge of the Philistine, they were stunned and terrified. (1 Samuel 17:10-11)

Goliath was the perfect bully—large, proud, dangerous ... and with a big mouth to boot. In his pride, Goliath made the mistake of insulting the armies of the living God. The proud always forget that it was God who made them large and dangerous to begin with. In their pride, they sometimes insult God Himself. David believed that God wanted him to defeat the giant, and though he was only a youth, he faced Goliath in battle. Goliath couldn't believe that a "mere boy" was challenging him to fight. Like any bully, Goliath laughed at David, taunting him.

He said to David, "Am I a dog that you come against me with a staff?" Then the Philistine cursed David by his gods and said to him, "Come here to me, and I will feed your flesh to the birds of the air and the beasts of the field."

David answered him: "You come against me with sword and spear and scimitar, but I come against you in the name of the LORD of hosts, the God of the armies of Israel whom you have insulted. Today the LORD shall deliver you into my hand; I will strike you down and cut off your head. This very day I will feed your dead body and the dead bodies of the Philistine army to the birds of the air and the beasts of the field; thus the whole land shall learn that Israel has a God. All this multitude, too, shall learn that it is not by sword or spear that the LORD saves. For the battle belongs to the LORD, who shall deliver you into our hands." (1 Samuel 17:43-47)

Goliath approached David, anxious to destroy him. David, however, loaded up a pebble and wound up his sling. He swung the sling ... around and around ... again and again ... until it reached a powerful rotational force, and he let it fly. With one shot, he took down the proud giant, and he cut off his head! As David said ... *the battle belongs to the Lord.*

Like the small stone in David's sling, the small beads of the Rosary slay the giants of darkness in today's world. God wants the proud to be humbled, and He often uses the simplest of instruments to humble them. Blessed James Alberione, founder of the Daughters of Saint Paul, said as much.[63] He said that Mary has used this mighty weapon of the Rosary to defeat Satan, just as David defeated the giant Goliath with a sling.

Mother Teresa always carried a Rosary with her. One day, when going through an airport security checkpoint, the guards asked if anyone had a weapon. To everyone's surprise, Mother Teresa raised her hand and said that she had a weapon! Suddenly, as everyone watched, she opened her hand, and revealed ... the Rosary.

We've seen the Rosary take on some pretty evil characters—Boko Haram and a serial killer. How does the rosary fare against a Satanic priest? Maybe you believe that your problems are too great to be solved ... that your problems are somehow different. Think again! I don't care who you are, what you've experienced, or how you've lived. Even if you're a Satanic priest, the Rosary can do great things for you.

---

[63] Calloway, *10 Wonders of the Rosary*, 29.

THE ROSARY MEETS A SATANIC PRIEST: THE STORY OF BARTOLO LONGO[64]

Bartolo Longo was born in 1841 to a wealthy family in southern Italy. Although he was raised a devout Catholic who prayed the Rosary daily, he decided to leave the faith while pursuing a law degree at the University of Naples. Bartolo became involved in a very strong anti-Catholic movement that was sweeping through the universities at that time. "I, too, grew to hate monks, priests and the Pope…" he would later write.

Bartolo began to frequent mediums in Naples, and over time, they gradually introduced him to the occult. Soon, he was attending séances, rituals and various occult practices. These activities only served to increase his desire. He eventually decided to be ordained a Satanic

---

[64] Angelo Stagnaro, "Blessed Bartolo Longo: The Ex-Satanist On the Path to Sainthood," *The Catholic Herald* (London), Jul. 19, 2011, accessed March 8, 2021; Fr. Roger J. Landry, "From Satanist to Saint," CatholiCity, October 31, 2008, accessed March 20, 2021, https://www.catholicity.com/commentary/landry/00691.html; Br. Ezra Sullivan, OP, "The Rosary: The Devil's Defeat," Catholic Exchange, October 26, 2007, accessed March 21, 2021, https://catholicexchange.com/the-rosary-the-devils-defeat.

priest. After a period of intense study and a rigorous fast, he was officially ordained, promising his soul to a demon. He presided over Satanic services and boldly spoke out against Christianity and Catholic influence; he convinced Catholics to leave the Church and join him in the occult.

However, over time, his life was marked by extreme sadness. He experienced paranoia, nervousness and deep depression. He was afflicted by diabolical visions. The torments of the demon eventually led him to mental breakdown.

In desperation, Bartolo sought the counsel of an old friend from his hometown, Professor Vincenzo Pepe. Pepe convinced him to abandon Satan, and he encouraged him to seek help from a Dominican priest, Father Alberto Radente. After several weeks and many long conversations, Father Radente gave Bartolo absolution and welcomed him back into the Church on the Feast of the Sacred Heart in 1865. Father Radente also encouraged Bartolo to consider the Rosary, and he inspired him with confidence in the power of Mary's intercession through this prayer.

However, Satan wasn't ready to let Bartolo go without a fight. Bartolo began to experience deep despair, and he considered suicide. As Bartolo considered his situation, his fear and depression only increased. As far as he knew, he was still consecrated to Satan, he was still Satan's property, and surely Satan awaited him in Hell! The more he considered these thoughts, the more he wanted to commit suicide. He then remembered the voice of Father Radente, repeating the words of the Blessed Mother: "One who propagates my Rosary shall be saved." Falling to his knees, he resolved at that moment that he would not leave earth without propagating the Rosary.

With that, Bartolo Longo began an amazing 180-degree turn in his life, a turn that has affected the lives of countless others throughout the last 150 years and still affects the lives of many today. To prove the sincerity of his conversion, Bartolo returned to his Satanist hangouts, but this time, he was wielding his Lightsaber, holding up a Rosary and publicly denouncing his former ways. He returned to his former abode, now ready to engage in spiritual warfare ... now ready to do some damage after the misery he had suffered at the hands of the Prince of Darkness! Bartolo walked into a séance and cried out: "I renounce spiritism because it is nothing but a maze of error and falsehood." At this point, Bartolo was strong enough to fight against Satan, and through the power of the Rosary, he appeared to have escaped Satan's clutches. (Bartolo's eventual beatification, noted below, is the Church's official confirmation that he is now in Heaven). He performed many good works, demonstrating that he had turned back to God and revealing that he had escaped Satan. In fact, through the Rosary, Bartolo was now attacking Satan. The tables had turned.

In an effort to make amends for his past life, Bartolo joined a charitable group. He helped orphans; he helped the poor. He wanted to dedicate his life to teaching others about Mary, praising her, and making her known and loved. Bartolo wrote books and pamphlets on catechesis, and he presented conferences on Christ's life and devotion to Mary. He founded many charitable institutions in Pompei, including a trade school, an orphanage, and a congregation of sisters to staff them. Pompei began to be known as the City of Mary due to the many buildings that Bartolo built.

Bartolo restored a dilapidated Catholic church and sponsored a feast in honor of Our Lady of the Rosary. He obtained an old painting of Mary, restored it, and installed it into his renovated church. Within hours after the installation, miracles began to be reported and many people came to the church. Seeing the attention the church was getting, the bishop of Nola encouraged Bartolo to build a larger church. The church was enlarged again and officially named *the Basilica of Our Lady of the Most Holy Rosary of Pompei* ... the only Catholic church in existence built by a former Satanic priest![65]

To spread devotion to Mary and the Rosary, Bartolo attended parties and local cafés, explaining the dangers of the occult. He continued promoting the Rosary until his death. Just before death, Bartolo was lying in bed, surrounded by the orphans he had worked to educate, praying the Rosary with them. After finishing, in his final

---

[65] Stagnaro, "Blessed Bartolo Longo."

breath, Bartolo expressed his sole desire ... to see Mary, who had saved him in the past and would now save him from the clutches of Satan.

Bartolo was buried in the basilica he had built. He was beatified by Pope John Paul II on October 26, 1980, with Pope John Paul calling him "the Apostle of the Rosary." More than thirty thousand people attended the ceremony. Approximately fifty thousand attended Pope Benedict's later visit to the basilica on October 9, 2008. About three million pilgrims visit the basilica every year. Bartolo has had a profound effect on the lives of countless poor, countless incurable patients, and so many abandoned orphans; he has inspired hope in the hopeless, and many miracles have been reported by those visiting his basilica. Hope has dawned in hearts that had given up as people have seen Mary's intercession and the power of the Rosary.

The beatification by Pope John Paul means that Bartolo is now in Heaven; in fact, he is now officially referred to as "Blessed Bartolo Longo." Thus, we see that Mary kept her promise, as she always does, interceding with her Son and obtaining eternal bliss for her servant Bartolo, who served her by spreading the Rosary.

It's rather amazing to see what a Spiritual Lightsaber can do ... even in the hands of a former Satanic priest! Now that Bartolo has slipped through Satan's grasp, what does Satan think about the power of the Rosary? Is he afraid of being beaten by it again? What do Satan and his demons have to say about this Spiritual Lightsaber?

DEMONS CONFESS THE POWER OF THE ROSARY DURING EXORCISMS

Now, we all know that Satan is the consummate liar, and the Bible makes this clear. So why should we listen to him? Jesus gave power to His disciples to perform exorcisms, granting them "power over unclean spirits" (Mark 6:7). Thus, we find Jesus' disciples performing exorcisms in His Name (Acts 8:7; Acts 16:18). I want to focus on the "Q & A session" during the exorcism, the point where the exorcist gets to ask the demon questions in Jesus' Name. Jesus' power forces the demon to leave the possessed person, and Jesus' power forces the demon to tell the truth. Jesus, working through His Church, grants the exorcist power over the demon when the exorcist invokes His Name; the exorcist calls upon this power to force demons to tell the truth.

What the demon divulges during an exorcism is absolutely incredible. The demon is humiliated when he is forced to reveal his most cherished secrets, his most prized schemes, his most closely held strategies for bringing souls to ruin. You can often tell that the exorcist hugely enjoys this part of the exorcism when listening to an audio recording of the exorcism, because, like a kid in a candy store, the exorcist can force the demon to reveal secrets at will.

Father Francesco Bamonte, a well-known exorcist in Italy, has written a book entitled *The Virgin Mary and the Devil in Exorcisms*, where he discusses what he and his colleagues have witnessed, and as I say, it is fascinating. Returning to my question, what does Satan himself have to say about the power of the Rosary?

I'll begin with my personal favorite.[66] Here, Father Bamonte is holding a Rosary in his hands during an exorcism, and the demon speaks. To paraphrase, the demon says that if we only knew it, he, the demon, would be destroyed in less than a second if we said the Rosary with faith. The demon then contemptuously rejects the Rosary in Father Bamonte's hands.

Keep in mind that the demon is speaking and acting through the possessed person. Thus, the possessed person, under the influence of a demon, is rejecting the Rosary with contempt. The demon says that he would be destroyed in less than a second ... amazing.

Another demon had this to say.[67]

---

[66] Fr. Francesco Bamonte, *The Virgin Mary and the Devil in Exorcisms*, 2nd English ed. (Libertyville, IL: Pope Leo XIII Institute Press, 2014), 111.

[67] Bamonte, *The Virgin Mary and the Devil in Exorcisms*, 111.

The demon said that our contemplation of the mysteries of the Rosary makes him sick. Our praying the Rosary is like striking him with blows. Furthermore, the Rosary takes so many souls away from him because it is a prayer of the Blessed Mother, referred to as "That One" by the demon.

The demons do not like to say the names of Jesus and Mary. In this case, the demon referred to Mary as "That One." The demon was forced to confess that the Rosary takes so many souls away from him .... amazing.

On another occasion, Father Bamonte put a Rosary around the neck of a possessed person, and this attracted the demon's attention very quickly.[68] At this, the demon attempted to tear off the Rosary from the neck of the possessed person, saying that whoever clings to the Rosary will never be lost.

Whoever clings to the Rosary will never be lost ... very encouraging! On another occasion, a demon confirmed the words of Padre Pio that I quoted at the beginning of this book. Padre Pio was a stigmatic priest (he bore Christ's wounds, the stigmata), and he strongly encouraged the Rosary, which he prayed unceasingly. Father Bamonte picked up a Rosary during an exorcism, and the following exchange ensued.[69]

---

[68] Bamonte, *The Virgin Mary and the Devil in Exorcisms*, 111.
[69] Bamonte, *The Virgin Mary and the Devil in Exorcisms*, 106-107.

The demon exclaimed that he couldn't stand the Rosary. He went on to say that a "stupid old person" appropriately referred to the Rosary as a "weapon," because it is truly a weapon against the demons. Father Bamonte then commanded the demon, in the Name of Jesus, to name the "stupid old man." The demon then said that this was Padre Pio!

Here, Father Bamonte, in Jesus' Name, forced the demon to tell him who the "stupid old man" was, and the demon named Padre Pio specifically. The demon was well acquainted with Padre Pio, and perhaps more amazing, the demon was even aware that Padre Pio had called the Rosary the weapon!

When I first encountered statements like these, I admit, it was tempting to believe that it was all too incredible to be true. However, these accounts are verified by other exorcists. Father Gabriele Amorth, who passed away in 2016, was the Chief Exorcist of the Vatican, and he documented similar exchanges with demons. Father Amorth lived an amazing life, and Hollywood has taken his story to the silver screen (*The Devil and Father Amorth*, 2018).

In his book *The Last Exorcist*, Father Amorth reports an entire dialogue that he had with the devil during one of his exorcisms. Here, I will concentrate on one particular statement Satan made. After the devil answers a series of questions posed by Father Amorth, we come to the following.[70]

Father Amorth recalls that during a particular exorcism, Satan, speaking through the possessed person, said that each Hail Mary is like taking a blow to the head for him. He added that if Christians understood the power of the Rosary, it would be the end of him.

If Christians understood the power of the Rosary, it would be THE END OF HIM. As revealed through exorcisms, Satan knows well who has been given the privilege of crushing his head, and he greatly fears Mary and the power of the Rosary. Why not place this time-tested weapon into your own arsenal? Why not place this powerful weapon into your own hands? Like a good Jedi, keep your Lightsaber strapped on at all times, ready at a moment's notice, come what may! Before I wrote this book, I never carried my Rosary. However, after doing the research for this book, I now carry it with me.

It is difficult to cover the power of the Rosary in a short book. Examples of its power span the centuries. I would like to conclude with several final examples.

---

[70] Gelsomino Del Guercio, "Devil admits to exorcist: 'I'm afraid of the Madonna,'" Aleteia, July 2, 2017, accessed March 15, 2021, https://aleteia.org/2017/07/02/devil-admits-to-exorcist-im-afraid-of-the-madonna/.

SISTER LUCIA, FATIMA VISIONARY: THERE'S NO PROBLEM THAT CANNOT BE SOLVED BY THE ROSARY

Such a statement, on the face of it, appears unbelievable, and did it not come from Sister Lucia, the eldest of the visionaries of Our Lady of Fatima (Mary's Church-approved apparitions from Portugal beginning in 1917), I would say that the statement is crazy.[71] Now, as with all prayer, God Himself determines what is good for His children, so this doesn't mean that Jesus will do whatever I ask. It does mean that the Rosary can obtain, by Mary's intercession, a God-given solution that will resolve the issue at hand. Keep in mind that Lucia is the eldest visionary of the Fatima apparitions, and she was blessed with personal apparitions of Mary. Lucia was a very important person, a holy woman sought out by popes and cardinals.

What did Lucia say?

According to Lucia, in the current times in which we

---

[71] Quoted in Antonio Socci, *The Fourth Secret of Fatima* (Fitzwilliam, NH: Loreto Publications, 2006), 97-101.

are living (which she calls the "last times"), the Blessed Virgin Mary has given a new power to the Holy Rosary, and this power is so great that there is no problem, no matter how difficult, be it temporal or above all, spiritual, that can't be resolved through the Rosary. This applies to problems in our private lives, in our families, in the families of the world, in religious communities, and in the life of peoples and nations.

For me, this is very consoling. Jesus told us to have confidence in the power of prayer (Mark 11:24; Matthew 7:7), and He appears to be especially receptive to the Rosary. Lucia passed away at age ninety-seven in 2005.

Lucia's statement sounds surprisingly broad in its application and coverage. Is the Rosary powerful enough to affect the world on a national or even a global scale?

THE BATTLE OF LEPANTO 1571: THE ROSARY DEFEATS ISLAM'S ATTEMPT TO TAKE EUROPE AND CONQUER ROME[72]

October 7 is the Feast of Our Lady of the Rosary, and it has been established to commemorate the sixteenth-century naval victory which many believe saved Europe from Turkish invasion. The Battle of Lepanto proved to be a perilous moment for Europe, and the outcome of this battle was decisive in determining the course of world history. Lepanto was the largest naval battle in Western history, including more than four hundred warships.[73] This victory is of the greatest importance in the history of Europe, and it marked a turning point in the expansion of the Ottoman Empire into the Mediterranean.[74]

A pivotal moment had arrived for Europe. The Muslim Turks were ravaging Eastern Europe, and in 1571, it appeared that the entire continent would fall to their

---

[72] Johnnette S. Benkovic and Thomas K. Sullivan, *The Rosary: Your Weapon for Spiritual Warfare* (Cincinnati: Franciscan Media, 2017), 4-9.

[73] "Battle of Lepanto," Wikipedia, last modified March 3, 2021, accessed March 28, 2021, https://en.wikipedia.org/wiki/Battle_of_Lepanto.

[74] Wikipedia, "Battle of Lepanto."

control. Many, including Pope Pius V, believed that this was a critical time, and he saw the advancement of the Turkish Ottoman Empire as a great threat to Christianity. Islam's goal was to take Europe and especially to conquer Rome itself. Once the Turks took Europe, the Pope knew they would be coming for him next. Pius V knew that this was a war with high stakes. The Pope formed the Holy League, an alliance of Catholic maritime forces, and he asked the faithful to pray the Rosary and beg for Mary's intercession.

The Pope chose the famous Don Juan of Austria to be the Holy League's general. Don Juan, though only twenty-four years old, was known to be a great swordsman, and he had distinguished himself in prior battles. As popular lore attests, Don Juan was handsome and sought after by the ladies. He was also deeply devoted to Mary. He knew when to use his sword, and he wielded it very effectively; however, he observed justice and prudence in his usage of power. Don Juan obediently followed the Pope's orders; women would not be allowed on the ship, blasphemy would not be allowed, and he invited the crew to join him in a three-day fast. Priests offered Mass and heard confessions. The Pope realized that this would be more than just a military battle; it would be a spiritual battle as well.

The sound of the Rosary filled the air on the night before the battle. The Holy League knelt on the galley decks, Rosaries in hand. Throughout the Italian peninsula and throughout Europe, the faithful filled the churches, and at the request of the Pope, they prayed the Rosary for victory. In the early morning hours of the day of battle, Mass was celebrated on the decks of the Holy League ships.

However, things did not look good for the Holy League. Hampered by mist, fog, and strong headwinds, they struggled to make their way through the choppy sea into the Gulf of Patras. As they rounded the corner, they could see the immense war galleys of the Ottoman Empire rising in the distance, set in full battle array. The ships were arrayed in a huge crescent, the symbol of Islam. The crescent was a terrifying sight to behold, silhouetted against the horizon ... poised for destruction.

As the Holy League approached, the men could see the battle pennant of Ali Pasha, the Muslim commander, flying from his ship's mast. After considering the situation, Don Juan decided to engage. He ordered the Holy League's battle pennant to be raised on his command flagship, the *Real*. As the banner unfurled, it revealed a huge picture of the crucified Christ. With Rosaries at the ready, the men implored the help of Mary as they made their final battle preparations.

At first, however, the winds were against the Holy League, and it was feared that the Turks would be able to make contact before a line of battle could be formed.[75] With the winds blowing against him, Don Juan raised his eyes to heaven, begging God to bless him with victory. The officers and men on the other ships followed suit.

Then ... what seemed like a miracle occurred; the headwinds changed direction, and they began to blow against the Muslim fleet.[76] The Holy League quickly raised its sails, and the Muslim fleet dropped theirs. With the wind at their backs, the Holy League moved in to attack.

Key to the victory was the all-out fight between the two flagships. Breaking with tradition, the leaders decided to directly engage. The *Real* flagship, commanded by Don Juan, and the *Sultana*, commanded by the Muslim commander Ali Pasha, collided with enormous force, and an all-out duel ensued. The crews engaged in hand-to-hand combat. It was a fight to the death with much bloodshed. The *Real* was nearly taken.[77] Once again, things did not look good for the Holy League. Would the *Real* fall into the enemy hands?

The Colonna fights back

During the fight, Don Juan was wounded. When it looked as if the *Real* might fall the Holy League ship *Colonna*

---

[75] Wikipedia, "Battle of Lepanto."
[76] Wikipedia, "Battle of Lepanto."
[77] Wikipedia, "Battle of Lepanto."

came alongside the *Real,* launching a counterattack.[78] The *Colonna* fought bravely, and with their help, the Turks were taken off the *Real*. The *Sultana* was then boarded, and the Holy League killed all of its crew, including Ali Pasha. Having captured the Muslim flagship, the Holy League hoisted the Holy League banner up its mast, in an effort to destroy the morale of the Turkish ships, to the sound of Christian cheers and cries of "Victory." Within two hours of fighting, the Turks were beaten "left and centre."[79]

Tradition has it that on that day, Pope Pius V interrupted a meeting with his cardinals and stepped aside to look out the window. With a privileged revelation, he suddenly told the cardinals that they should set aside business and pray on their knees, giving God thanksgiving for the great victory He had given the fleet that day.

We've seen the Rosary save lives and help in a major battle. How does the power of the Rosary hold up in a more common need, such as the search for a future spouse?

---

[78] Wikipedia, "Battle of Lepanto."
[79] Wikipedia, "Battle of Lepanto."

JACKIE FRANCOIS'
SEARCH FOR A HUSBAND:
THE ROSARY NOVENA[80]

My final example is more personal. World events are certainly important, and I'm impressed by the Battle of Lepanto. Nevertheless, we are often more impressed by day-to-day needs than we are by life-and-death struggles. In the examples above, the Rosary has proven itself a trusty and reliable weapon against evil and danger. How does it fare with an "everyday need," like the search for a spouse?

Jackie presents her story on YouTube. It's fabulous, and it inspired me; in fact, it made my day.

About ten years before Jackie made her novena, her friend's mother gave her a little blue novena booklet, the type of booklet people often forget. You might accept it more to satisfy the giver than anything else. Your grandmother might have given you one, or maybe

---

[80] Jackie Francois Angel, *"How God Answered My Prayer,"* Ascension Presents, September 24, 2019, video, accessed November 14, 2021, https://youtu.be/AlK_bJqEEU0.

your uncle did. Nevertheless, these novenas can be very powerful, and I must confess that I never suspected how powerful they can be. I now have much greater respect for those "little blue booklets."

First, some background. What is a Rosary novena? Novena means nine, so a Rosary novena means praying the Rosary on nine consecutive days. These novenas come in various flavors; some are said for nine days, some for twenty-seven days (three novenas), and some for fifty-four days (six novenas). Often, they have accompanying prayers. The key is that you pray the Rosary on nine consecutive days for a particular intention. That's the central part of this devotion.

There is a private revelation associated with the fifty-four-day novena, in which Mary appeared to recommend this practice to Fortuna Agrelli, a sick woman in Italy.[81] For thirteen months, Fortuna had suffered terribly from sickness and was very near death. Physicians had given up hope. On February 16, 1884, Fortuna and her family began a novena of Rosaries, calling out in desperation to the Queen of Heaven. On March 3, Mary appeared to Fortuna in great beauty, holding the Child Jesus on her lap and in her hand, a Rosary.

---

[81] Chris Hallenbeck, *The Miraculous 54 Day Rosary Novena to Our Lady* (Gloversville, NY: Great Point Publishing, 2019), 2-3.

Mary told Fortuna that she was pleased to be invoked by the title of "Queen of the Holy Rosary," and that with this invocation, she could no longer refuse Fortuna's request, since this title is precious and dear to her. Mary advised Fortuna to make three novenas, adding that in this way, she would obtain all. Later, Mary said, *Whoever desires to obtain favors from me should make three novenas of the prayers of the Rosary, and three novenas in thanksgiving.* Fortuna and her family completed the six novenas, and she was restored to perfect health.

Jackie prayed the 54 day rosary novena for friends and family and experienced some amazing successes, but her search for a husband was unsuccessful. She had dated several guys, none of whom had worked out. However, as the Bible recommends (Luke 11:8; Matthew 15:21-28), Jackie decided to persevere. In Matthew 15, the Canaanite woman's persevering faith eventually won the day; Jesus performed a miracle for her, rewarding her faith. Jackie decided to try the rosary novena again, this time praying for a husband, "wherever he was." She planned to end the novena on the feast day of the Assumption, August 15, a very special Marian feast. At that time, she had no clue who her future husband might be. Jackie was tempted to quit, tempted to give up on this prayer effort. It was obviously difficult (54 days), and it had not resulted in a husband. Personally, I believe that the novena may have prevented her from marrying the wrong guy, but nevertheless, she was still single. Despite the temptation to quit, she refused to give up and pressed on.

This time, as fate would have it, she met a guy, meeting him the very next day, on June 24th. She was very excited about Bobby, and her expectations were high. The relationship appeared to go surprisingly well. However, on day fifty four, they were still dating. She couldn't help but wonder, why didn't something happen? Was engagement a future prospect? Jackie emphasizes that the 54 day rosary novena isn't a magical formula. This is just another way of persevering in prayer, using a prayer that Mary has specifically requested. Jackie couldn't see any direct result to her prayers, but as before, she decided to hold onto her faith and keep praying.

Fifty-four days later, as Jackie wondered about the success of her prayers, something was happening, something momentous, but it was hidden from her eyes. Fifty-four days later, on August 15, unbeknownst to Jackie, Bobby bought an engagement ring! Three months later, he proposed. Jackie and Bobby are now married with three children.

What is the conclusion of this story? Persist! Take up the 54 day rosary novena, calling on the Queen of Heaven to intercede with her Son, until you get an answer! This is yet another example of P.U.S.H. (Pray Until Something Happens). Secondly, just because you don't see results happening, doesn't mean they are not there! Jesus will test your faith and your perseverance, but if you hold steady, you'll obtain something fabulous.

Jackie emphasizes that God is unpredictable; He may answer in the way that you ask, or He may answer in a completely different way. He might not seem to answer at all. We all want an answer, but God wants more; He often sees that there is something even better for us.

In addition to the numerous blessings the Popes have attached to it, Mary appeared to Saint Dominic promising fifteen specific blessings to those who pray the Rosary. As I list these, I want to emphasize that Mary only does what her Son wants. Mary would not appear to Saint Dominic unless Jesus asked her to. I also want to emphasize that praying, reading Scripture and meditating on the mysteries of our Redemption are central to being a Christian. Thus, it is not surprising that Mary would encourage us to engage in these activities, as these are the main activities of the Rosary. I recommend watching Mel Gibson's *The Passion of the Christ* movie while praying the Sorrowful mysteries, as this meditation has greatly helped me.

THE 15 PROMISES
OF THE ROSARY[82]

1. *Whoever shall faithfully serve me by the recitation of the Rosary, shall receive signal graces.*

2. *I promise my special protection and the greatest graces to all those who shall recite the Rosary.*

3. *The Rosary shall be a powerful armor against hell, it will destroy vice, decrease sin, and defeat heresies.*

4. *The Rosary will cause virtue and good works to flourish; it will obtain for souls the abundant mercy of God; it will withdraw the hearts of men from the love of the world and its vanities, and will lift them to the desire for eternal things. Oh, that souls would sanctify themselves by this means.*

5. *The soul which recommends itself to me by the recitation of the Rosary, shall not perish.*

6. *Whoever shall recite the Rosary devoutly, applying himself to the consideration of its sacred mysteries shall never be conquered by misfortune. God will not chastise him in His justice, he shall not perish by an unprovided death; if he be just he shall remain in the grace of God, and become worthy of eternal life.*

---

[82] "The 15 Promises of the Blessed Virgin Mary to Catholics who pray the Rosary everyday," accessed October 18, 2021, www.rosarypromises.com.

7. *Whoever shall have a true devotion for the Rosary shall not die without the sacraments of the Church.*

8. *Those who are faithful to recite the Rosary shall have during their life and at their death the light of God and the plenitude of His graces; at the moment of death they shall participate in the merits of the saints in paradise.*

9. *I shall deliver from Purgatory those who have been devoted to the Rosary.*

10. *The faithful children of the Rosary shall merit a high degree of glory in Heaven.*

11. *You shall obtain all you ask of me by the recitation of the Rosary.*

12. *All those who propagate the Holy Rosary shall be aided by me in their necessities.*

13. *I have obtained from my Divine Son that all the advocates of the Rosary shall have for intercessors the entire celestial court during their life and at the hour of death.*

14. *All who recite the Rosary are my sons and daughters, and brothers and sisters of my only Son Jesus Christ.*

15. *Devotion of my Rosary is a great sign of predestination.*

Note that promise number two includes Mary's special protection. We see a lot of Mary's special protection in the stories above. In promise number two, Mary also states that those who recite the Rosary will receive the greatest graces ... not just graces, but the greatest graces! Truly, who can turn down these blessings!

Before leaving this topic, I quote several advocates of the Rosary. My personal favorite is Padre Pio, who said, *The Rosary is THE weapon.*

Advocate	Context	Quote
Our Lady of Fatima[83]	Mary appeared to three shepherd children in Fatima, Portugal in 1917, in a Church-approved apparition.	*Continue to pray the Rosary every day.*
Saint Francis de Sales[84]	Famous saint and Doctor of the Church.	*The greatest method of praying is to pray the Rosary.*
Pope Blessed Pius IX[85]	Promulgated the dogma of the Immaculate Conception.	*Give me an army saying the Rosary and I will conquer the world.*
Saint Louis de Montfort[86]	Famous for spreading the Rosary, author of The Secret of the Rosary.	*Never will anyone who says his Rosary every day be led astray. This is a statement that I would gladly sign with my blood.*
Padre Pio[87]	Priest who bore the Stigmata.	*The rosary is THE weapon.*

---

[83] TFP Student Action, "Best 19 Quotes on the Rosary."
[84] TFP Student Action, "Best 19 Quotes on the Rosary."
[85] TFP Student Action, "Best 19 Quotes on the Rosary."
[86] TFP Student Action, "Best 19 Quotes on the Rosary."
[87] TFP Student Action, "Best 19 Quotes on the Rosary."

How have I been affected by writing this book? Before researching the Rosary, I was struggling to finish one 5-decade Rosary a day. After completing the book, I now pray three 5-decade Rosaries a day. I say this not to brag, but to highlight the effect of everything I have learned. There are many, many stories on the power of the Rosary, but I can't cover them all.

Before I wrote this book, if someone told me they were praying three Rosaries a day, I would have thought they were a little crazy, a little overzealous. Now, however, I completely understand. I was amazed by the stories I encountered, and they inspired me to pray the Rosary more frequently. I started to do this during Lent of 2021. As Lent came to a close, I was experiencing a big sense of peace; the peace was wonderful. Jackie Angel's story moved me so much that I started my own fifty-four-day Rosary novena. Hopefully, in a later edition of this book, I can tell you what happens. It is my hope that you too can experience the peace that I have felt from this prayer.

WARRIORS FOR MARY

Mary is looking for a Few Good Warriors. Will you Answer Her Request?

Our Lady of Fatima noted that many souls are lost because they have no one to make sacrifices and pray for them. Mary has asked that people pray the rosary every day to prevent the loss of souls. This is the purpose of Warriors for Mary, (1) to greatly help you get closer to Jesus, (2) to help you reach Heaven and (3) to save the souls of your generation. While working to save the souls of your brothers and sisters, you will be greatly improving your own personal relationship with Jesus. You will be working to increase your inner peace, even during exterior difficulty in your life.

Warriors For Mary Requests: (details at **www. warriorsformary.com**)

Spend Two Weeks Doing Five Decades a Day (after two weeks, it will become easier, but don't take my word for it). If you need to start with ten minutes a day, doing two or three decades, start there, but stick with it. Prayer can be awkward at first, but it will grow on you.

After 2 Weeks, Continue Each Day. Five decades will take twenty minutes a day.

Persist. The devil will work against you, because he hates the rosary. He's admitted as much (in exorcisms) because he knows the rosary steals souls from him (see "Demons Confess the Power of the Rosary During Exorcisms" above).

Support Each Other. You will form a Battalion with several or more of your friends. Support the members of your Battalion. This is a battle for the souls in your generation.

Receive Monthly Confession. The rosary will help you to see any sins in your life in a whole new way. Monthly Confession will do wonders for your relationship with Jesus and your peace of soul.

Visit Jesus in the Tabernacle for 30 Minutes Monthly. He wants to talk with you, one-on-one, about what is going on with you. He will give you the strength that only He can give. If you need help believing that He is really present, re-read the section on Eucharistic miracles.

Attend Daily Mass Twice a Month, on the First Friday and First Saturday of each month. There are two reasons for this: (1) we need the strength of Jesus in the

Eucharist and (2) we want to receive the promise of the First Friday and First Saturday devotions. What are these? In private revelations, Jesus and Mary appeared to ask for reparation for sin. They requested specific actions of reparation, including primarily the worthy reception of Holy Communion on the First Friday and First Saturday of every month. In return, Jesus and Mary promised graces of salvation. I provide details below.

First Friday Devotion: Jesus appeared to Saint Margaret Mary Alacoque in 1673 on multiple occasions, and these apparitions were later approved by the Church. On one occasion, Jesus said the following:[88]

In the excess of the mercy of my heart, I promise you that my all powerful love will grant to all those who will receive Communion on the First Fridays, for nine consecutive months, the grace of final repentance: they will not die in my displeasure, nor without receiving the sacraments; and my Heart will be their secure refuge in that last hour.

How does one fulfill this request?

On the first Friday of nine consecutive months:

1. Receive Holy Communion on each of the First

---

[88] "1st Friday & 1st Saturday Devotions." America Needs Fatima. Accessed June 26, 2022. https://americaneedsfatima.org/blog/1st-friday-1st-saturday-devotions.

Fridays;

2. The nine first Fridays must be consecutive;

3. They must be made in honor of and in reparation to His Sacred Heart (form this intention in your mind and heart while receiving Communion).

Jesus' promise above is unbelievably fabulous. A complete explanation of this is beyond the scope of this book. Keep in mind that attending mass on nine consecutive First Fridays will require focus. Fortunately, I completed mine recently, but sure enough one of the First Fridays was Good Friday, and I had to hustle to make the only mass offered that day at 3pm. Like I said, this will require focus. Many parishes offer an evening mass on First Friday to accommodate those making this devotion, but you'll need to do some homework to get details.

First Saturday Devotion: During Mary's third apparition in her Church approved appearances at Fatima, on July 13, 1917, she said that she would later return to request the Communion of Reparation of the First Five Saturdays. In December of 1925, Mary appeared to Sister Lucia, making this request.

See, my daughter, My Heart surrounded with thorns with which ingrates pierce me at every moment with blasphemies and ingratitude. You, at least, make sure to console me and announce that all those who for five months, on the first

Saturdays, go to confession, receive Communion, say five decades of the Rosary and keep me company for 15 minutes meditating on the mysteries of the Rosary, with the purpose of making reparation to Me, I promise to assist them at the hour of death with all the graces necessary for the salvation of their souls.

How does one fulfill this request?

On the first Saturday of five consecutive months:

1. Go to confession;
2. Receive Holy Communion;
3. Say five decades of the Rosary;
4. Keep Our Lady company for 15 minutes, meditating on the mysteries of the Rosary.

Have the intention of making reparation for offenses committed towards her. These offenses include blasphemies against her (a) Immaculate Conception, (b) virginity and (c) divine maternity, as well as (d) actions of those who instill indifference towards her motherhood in the hearts of children and (e) insults against her sacred images. The Five First Saturdays correspond with these five offenses. In May of 1930, Jesus revealed this to Sister Lucia.

Note that you do not have to meditate on all of the mysteries of the rosary; you may meditate on several or even one if you choose.

Ask Mary for Help!!! She will lead you to Jesus, which is her sole purpose in life. And she is very good at it. Her favorite words, when speaking about her Son, are *Do whatever he tells you.* (John 2:5) She is the woman promised in Genesis! The woman who, by Jesus' grace and power, will crush Satan's head! She wants you to take part in this victory.

Read the 15 Promises of the Rosary (given by Mary to St. Dominic). These are incredible, and many, many people have seen them fulfilled (see the stories above). But persistence (often lots of persistence) is required.

Again, Support Each Other. The United States Navy Seals, one of the most effective fighting forces in the world, always refer to themselves as the "Seals Teams." The Seals are effective because they have learned to work as a team. We go up or down as a team, working together. Your friends need you, and you need them. Work as a unit. Support each other. Your generation is depending on you.

Know That This Effort Will Immensely Help You Get to Heaven. You will be reading Scripture and meditating on the mysteries of the Bible. This will help you immensely in your relationship with Jesus. Mary has promised this in Promise #2 above: *The soul which recommends itself to me by the recitation of the rosary, shall not perish.*

Remember the words of Our Lady of Fatima: *Pray the*

rosary every day.

Remember the words of Saint Padre Pio, who bore the stigmata: *The rosary is the weapon that wins all battles*.

You are called Warriors, because, by Jesus' grace, Warriors steal souls from Satan. Take Mary up on her request. Take up your Spiritual Lightsaber, and watch her obtain the "greatest graces" from her Son. She's promised the greatest graces through the rosary, because Jesus asked her to promise this (Promise #2 above).

Offer to Lead a Family Rosary in Your Home. This can make a huge difference. You have no idea how powerful this prayer can be when prayed in union with the members of your family. My grandfather did this when he was staying with us, and my sister and I joined in.

Pray fifteen Minutes of Conversational Prayer, one on one with Jesus, daily. This prayer is a simple conversation between you and Jesus, and I explain it below. Start out with five minutes a day. I describe this conversation in the IF TODAY YOU HEAR HIS VOICE section, toward the end of the book.

Creed of The Warriors For Mary:

The daily Rosary is a big deal.

Why?

Because Mary asked for it.

Why?

Because Jesus wanted her to.

Why?

To save the souls of our generation.

IF TODAY YOU HEAR HIS VOICE...TALKING ONE ON ONE WITH JESUS

For he is our God, we are the people he shepherds, the sheep in his hands. Oh, that today you would hear his voice. (Psalm 95:7)

My sheep hear my voice ... (John 10:27)

The Rosary is incredibly powerful, and I always recommend it. In addition, I recommend that you converse with Jesus one on one, expressing feelings, thoughts and sentiments in your own words. The saints have strongly recommended this. In this bonus section, I cover this one on one conversation between you and Jesus. You heard me correctly; this is a one on one conversation between you and Jesus. You will be engaged in a real conversation with Him, but it isn't necessarily audible. People have engaged in this personal conversation for centuries. I must practice what I preach; I pray my Rosary and engage in this one on one conversation every day. ... *Oh that today you would hear his voice.* (Psalm 95:7) Why would the Bible say this, unless you could actually hear God's voice (again, not necessarily audibly)? Furthermore, as John 10:3 says, He calls his sheep … By Name … personally. … *and the sheep hear his voice, as he calls his own sheep by name and leads them out.* (John 10:3)

You can engage in this conversation anytime and anywhere, although I recommend that you do so in front of the Tabernacle if possible. I recommend the Tabernacle, because Jesus is present there in the Eucharist (see section on Eucharistic miracles which supports this). However, if the Tabernacle is not available, any quiet place will do. In this section I explain the conversation and provide examples, but keep in mind that this is a personal conversation between you and Jesus. I can provide guidelines, but at the end of day, you determine what you want to say to Him.

Jesus often calls to people, and they don't hear what He is saying. They can't hear through the noise, the emails, the voice mails, the text messages, the events … the never ending activity of our modern world. You will need to escape this temporarily to achieve the silence that will enable you to hear what He is saying to you. Remember He is the Son of God, the Lord. This is a conversation you won't want to miss.

An Unbelievable Story: Pope Francis' Open Audience After World Youth Day 2016

In 2016, World Youth Day was held in Krakow, Poland, from July 25-31, and not surprisingly, it was a wonderful experience for youth from all over the world. World Youth Day (WYD) is a worldwide encounter with the Pope, typically celebrated in a different country every three years. On this particular occasion, Pope Francis did something that none of his predecessors have done; he offered an open audience to any of the faithful. As World Youth Day finished, Pope Francis made himself available to any youth that might want to come and personally visit, ask him questions, or just spend time with him. Yes, you could just walk right in and talk to him. This was a very unusual offer, and at first, the Vatican wasn't sure what to make of it. Nevertheless, they didn't want to discourage Pope Francis' apostolic spirit, so they went with it.

As it turned out, the occasion turned out to be an embarrassment for Pope Francis, and fortunately, it received very little press. Even though teens could walk right in and speak with him, very few showed up. Perhaps more insulting, people would walk by his room without even stopping in to say hi. People were anxious to get back home, anxious to do some sight-seeing, anxious to do so many things that people have to do today. Pope Francis was humbled, and even though he carried it off with a papal smile, inside, he was hurt by the event. It's rare that a Pope offers a papal audience, and rarer still, without an appointment. Yet the Pope often found himself alone, without visitors.

Now, I must confess. I actually made up this story, but I did so to make a point. It is shocking to believe that anyone would turn down an audience with the Pope. It is almost inconceivable that anyone would refuse to take time out of their busy schedule to see the leader of the Catholic Church, the Vicar of Christ on Earth. In fact, people wait a long time to find an opportunity to meet one on one with the Pope, and they might never succeed. Nevertheless, even more astonishing, is the fact that the Creator of the Universe, the Son of God, the Lord of Heaven and Earth, is sitting in Tabernacles at this very moment, alone, without visitors. Anyone can visit him. Anyone can speak with him... without an appointment, without permission, and without waiting. He makes himself available 24/7, day or night, at your local Catholic church. However, few take him up on this offer. Thus, the King of the Universe offers an audience, to an empty church, an empty chapel, and an empty room.

Even the people in ancient Israel did not have it so good. When Jesus walked the streets of Jerusalem, people waited to see him. They had to fight crowds, find out where he was and hope his disciples would let them in. In fact, in the Gospel, we find people lowering a man through a roof to reach Jesus (Matthew 9:2-8). If you did succeed in getting to Him, your time was limited, as He would soon need to be off to the next town. Today, however, you have all the time in the world to visit him.

John answered them, "I baptize with water; but there is one among you whom you do not recognize..." (John 1:26)

John the Baptist could repeat today what he said to the Israelites 2000 years ago, *there is one among you whom you do not recognize,* one among you, far closer than you would ever imagine, right in the Tabernacle. Jesus performs Eucharistic miracles, and He makes himself available, because he wants to talk to us. He waits, hours and hours in the Tabernacle, hoping that we will visit and tell him what's going on in our lives. What happened at the party you never expected to go to, what's happening with your friends right now, what's going on with your family- He wants to hear all about it. He made himself a "prisoner" in the Tabernacle so that you can come to Him and talk about what's going on. Oh that today you would hear his voice. Most of us, however, do not recognize Him.

To be at the service of others does not only mean to be ready for action. It means also to be in conversation with God with an attitude of listening, just like Mary. (Pope Francis, VIDEO MESSAGE TO YOUNG PEOPLE ON THE OCCASION OF THE 34th WORLD YOUTH DAY 2019)

To be in conversation with God Pope Francis has said. Why would Jesus go to the trouble of creating Eucharistic Miracles? Why is He trying hard, really hard, to get your attention? He obviously wants you to believe in His Real Presence in the Eucharist. The bloody Host expresses the torture Jesus underwent to endure His passion and save us from our sins. Jesus wants you to believe in Eucharistic miracles not just as an exercise in faith, not so you can check a box or pass a Catechism exam. He is looking for a lot more. He is looking for a personal connection with you. He wants you to personally appreciate and understand what he has suffered for you, and He wants a relationship with you. As God, He doesn't need anything, and He doesn't need us in any particular capacity. However, He chooses to want us intensely.

When I was a teen preparing for Confirmation, I often asked myself, does God know me? Does He really know me by name? I used to wonder, how is it that people 2000 years ago could speak with Jesus, but I'm unable to do so now? Am I being penalized for having been born after Jesus ascended into Heaven? Actually, I can visit Jesus in the Tabernacle any time I want. This is a God who knows me by name. A God Who waits for my personal visit. If you're not sure that Jesus is in the Tabernacle, please read the section on Eucharistic Miracles where you will find scientific evidence of this.

But what happens after that? Assuming you do come to a belief in His Real Presence, what happens next? This is what I want to focus on in this chapter, because what happens next is what's most important. Knowledge is great, but Relationship is so much more than knowledge. Knowing who Jesus is requires a lot more than knowing facts about Jesus.

Think about a close friend for a moment. After you learned something about him, you started to interact with him, talk with him and spend time with him. Wasn't that much more satisfying than just knowing about him? In the case of your friend, you've gone beyond knowledge to having a relationship with him.

Jesus, dying on the Cross, in one of His final statements, says... *I thirst.* (John 19:28) He is going through His final agony. He is undergoing the horrific suffering captured in the tissue samples found in the Eucharistic miracles, captured by modern science (see section on Eucharistic miracles). Yet, as many saints have suggested, even in His horrific agony, He is not experiencing physical thirst primarily. He is thirsting for a relationship with each one of us. He wants you to go beyond knowledge to having a relationship with Him. Actually, more – in His bitter agony as He is dying, He is thirsting for this relationship.

How does this relationship work? In some ways, it's very similar to the relationship you have with your close friend. Just as you spend time with your friend, Jesus wants you to "spend time" with Him. This can happen in a number of ways. You might, for example, go to your friend's house. In Jesus' case, you would go to the church and sit in front of the tabernacle and talk to Him. You can speak with Jesus anywhere actually.

Before getting into the details, though, I remember how the teens in my Catechism class responded when I first suggested that Jesus wanted to talk with them. They were happy with the idea, but they couldn't believe me, and they pressed me to prove it. I attempt to do so now.

Does our faith teach a personal God, who wants to talk one on one with you? What does the Bible say?

Reference	Quote	My Thoughts
Revelation 3:20	*Behold, I stand at the door and knock. If anyone hears my voice and opens the door, [then] I will enter his house and dine with him, and he with me.* **Revelation 3:20 USCCB**	"I will enter his house and dine with him, and he with me." It's obvious that this is one on one. "And he with me." And Jesus says...anyone. Not Moses, Abraham or Saint Paul... And Jesus is the one knocking at the door! The King of Kings is knocking at your door!

Reference	Quote	My Thoughts
Psalm 95: 7-8	*For he is our God, we are the people he shepherds, the sheep in his hands. Oh, that today you would hear his voice: Do not harden your hearts as at Meribah, as on the day of Massah in the desert.* **Psalm 95 7-8 USCCB**	"Oh that today you would hear his voice...." Not just David or Moses or Saint Paul....but you, as it says specifically (not necessarily audibly). Because He wants to speak to you.
John 10:27	*My sheep hear my voice; I know them, and they follow me.* **John 10:27 USCCB**	My sheep hear my voice. From Christ Himself. Not any voice, but my voice. Again, not necessarily audibly.
Matthew 6:6	*But when you pray, go to your inner room, close the door, and pray to your Father in secret. And your Father who sees in secret will repay you.* **Matthew 6:6 USCCB**	Inner room. Implies a private conversation. Privacy. Intimacy. One on One.

Reference	Quote	My Thoughts
Matthew 17:5	*While he was still speaking, behold, a bright cloud cast a shadow over them, then from the cloud came a voice that said, "This is my beloved Son, with whom I am well pleased; listen to him."* **Matthew 17:5 USCCB**	Listen to Him. Why? Because He's trying to speak with you.
John 15:15	*I no longer call you slaves, because a slave does not know what his master is doing. I have called you friends, because I have told you everything I have heard from my Father.* **John 15:15 USCCB**	I have called you friends. Friends have conversation together.

What do you do with your close friends? You have conversation together. What do the saints say on this topic? Do they support the interpretation I'm suggesting? Hugely so, saying that this one on one conversation with Christ is not only real, but in fact, it is central to our salvation.

Saint/ Speaker	Quote	My Thoughts
St Teresa of Avila (Doctor)	*Contemplative prayer [oración mental] is nothing else than a close sharing between friends; it means taking time frequently to be alone with him who we know loves us[89].*	A close sharing between friends.
St Teresa of Avila (Doctor)	*Friendly dealing, many times dealing one-on-one with Him whom we know loves us. And this person has a face which we can contemplate, a face that is a singular manifestation of his person.[90]*	Personal, one on one.

---

[89] "Mental Prayer." The Spiritual Life. Accessed July 17, 2022. https://slife.org/mental-prayer/
[90] The Spiritual Life, "Mental Prayer."

Saint/ Speaker	Quote	My Thoughts
St Alphonsus Liguori (Doctor)	*...All the saints have become saints by mental prayer[91].*	You'll be in good company. (This conversational prayer is often called "mental prayer," to distinguish it from prayers that are typically vocal, where particular words are recited, such as the Our Father prayer).
St Francis De Sales (Doctor)	*I commend earnest mental prayer to you, more particularly such as bears upon the Life and Passion of our Lord. If you contemplate Him frequently in meditation, your whole soul will be filled with Him, you will grow in His Likeness, and your actions will be molded on His[92].*	You become like the friends that you converse with, and so it is when you converse with Jesus.

---

[91] The Spiritual Life, "Mental Prayer."
[92] The Spiritual Life, "Mental Prayer."

Saint/ Speaker	Quote	My Thoughts
Joseph Ratzinger (who became Pope Benedict the XVI)	*[Sanctity is] nothing other than to speak with God as a friend speaks with a friend, allowing God to work, the Only One who can really make the world both good and happy*[93].	As a friend speaks with a friend.
The Franciscan Friars Minor	*Mental prayer is not just for priests and nuns, but is for everyone. The youngest of children are capable of reaching great heights through mental prayer*[94].	For everyone.
Mother Teresa (St. Teresa of Calcutta)	*We must never forget that we are bound to perfection and should aim ceaselessly for it. The practice of mental prayer is necessary to reach that goal. Because it is the breath of life for our soul, holiness is impossible without it*[95].	Breath of life for our soul.

---

[93] The Spiritual Life, "Mental Prayer."
[94] The Spiritual Life, "Mental Prayer."
[95] The Spiritual Life, "Mental Prayer."

Saint/ Speaker	Quote	My Thoughts
St Alphonsus Liguori (Doctor)	*It is morally impossible for him who neglects meditation to live without sin[96].*	Necessary to avoid sin.
St Teresa of Avila (Doctor)	*He who neglects mental prayer needs no devil to carry him to hell. He brings himself there with his own hands[97].*	Not only does Jesus talk with us personally, but in fact, we need this conversation.
St John of the Cross (Doctor)	*Without the aid of mental prayer, the soul cannot triumph over the forces of the demon[98].*	If you stop speaking with a friend, what happens to your relationship with them? And there is no more important friend than Christ.

How long have you ever waited in line to see a famous athlete or celebrity or to get a signature? You might wait a long time for a famous actor or soccer star. Oddly enough, Jesus, the Creator of the Universe, is waiting in line to talk to you. Waiting in line, behind whatever else is there in front of him. Keep in mind, that Jesus was famous for conversing with sinners (see, among other passages,

[96] The Spiritual Life, "Mental Prayer."
[97] The Spiritual Life, "Mental Prayer."
[98] The Spiritual Life, "Mental Prayer."

Matthew 9:10-13). So no matter who you are, He wants to talk to you!

This Might Be Hard to Believe

What does Jesus want to talk about, you might ask? Can He explain why good people suffer? He wants to hear your doubts. Why hasn't He solved a problem in my family? He wants you to take your problem to him. Does He understand what I'm going through? He of all people understands, because He is God. He knows the past, the future and everything in between. Whatever doubt, concern, disbelief, question or anything else you have, He wants to hear about it! If you're having difficulty believing He's there, tell Him. If you're not sure you agree with what He says, tell Him. If you're not comfortable with any of this ... tell Him. Wherever you are in your faith, start the conversation. Although He waits for you to begin this conversation, remember He is not a passive God; He actively pursues you. Nevertheless, He will never take away your free will. As you read this text, I believe that He is pursuing you right now.

He is the Son of God. It's impossible to predict what He might say to you. Maybe He has allowed you to have a seemingly unsolvable problem, so that you will come to him for help. Again, he's God, so no one can limit Him, put Him in a box, or guess what He might say. Sometimes people don't approach Him until they have an impossible problem.

Jesus Wants This Conversation with *EVERYONE*

In John 4:7-26, Jesus carries on a rather unusual conversation with a woman at a well. Just in case you might be wondering, "Does Jesus want to talk with me?!" the Gospel of John shows Jesus reaching out to a complete stranger, someone known to be a "public sinner." In fact, the Pharisees often complained that Jesus *welcomes sinners and eats with them.* (Luke 15:2) Jesus purposely sought out sinners, so He wants to talk to everyone, and yes that means everyone.

How does this conversation unfold? Jesus arrives at a well, tired and thirsty. A Samaritan woman is there, and Jesus asks her for a drink. A conversation ensues, and as it proceeds, the woman realizes that Jesus is a prophet. At this point, she brings up questions, personal questions that she has about the faith. She tells Jesus directly what's on her mind, including questions she has. This is a direct conversation, in which each side communicates their concerns. The Samaritan woman is concerned about the right place to worship God (in Jerusalem or elsewhere) and Jesus is concerned that she will be thirsty again (and not receive "living water" or the Holy Spirit, Whom Jesus wants to offer). Jesus is also concerned that she doesn't understand the God she is worshiping. Finally, she asks for living water, and Jesus points out that she has to first correct a fault against the Ten Commandments, which in her case is living with someone outside of marriage. Finally, Jesus identifies Himself as the Messiah. I have always been particularly impressed with the faith of the Samaritan woman, as she knew that the Messiah would arrive ... *I know that the Messiah is coming* ... (John 4:25). Her faith was so strong that Jesus came and introduced Himself... personally. He wants to do the same with you.

This is a wonderful, Biblical example of a conversation with Jesus. I highly recommend that you read the passage, as it is filled with insights. Notice that this conversation is completely natural, with the woman being herself, listening and responding to Jesus' promptings. Notice also that Jesus allayed her fears and questions. This conversation was very fruitful, as the woman learned what Jesus wanted to teach her. The woman was so excited about having met Jesus that she forgot all about her reason for coming to the well in the first place, and she leaves her water jar there.

What Does this Conversation Look Like?

Here I provide an actual example. The teens in my class told me that this conversation seemed a bit awkward at first. Even with your close friends, conversation runs into dry spells. One of the best ways to deal with this is to have a favorite spiritual book or Bible handy, and keep reading until something moves you to speak. This is what Saint Teresa of Avila did. I can almost guarantee you that something will move you and spark a conversation.

Here I demonstrate the basics. I want to emphasize that there is no strict formula, and this is primarily a conversation between you and Jesus! It's not technical and it's not complicated... just a natural conversation.

1. I find a passage in Scripture that catches my attention. For me, it is Genesis 18:10-14. Here, God tells Abraham that he will have a son, even though he and his wife Sarah are extremely old and Sarah is barren. Overhearing this, Sarah laughs, because she finds it impossible to believe. I have also found it hard to believe that the Lord can help sometimes, so I imagine the scene (and read several earlier verses to get some context). I go to a quiet, private place, which for me is usually my room, but it could be the chapel, a field, a forest, etc. The Lord prefers to speak in silence (see 1 Kings 19:11-13 or Jesus praying alone in deserted places.)

   But the LORD said to Abraham: "Why did Sarah laugh and say, 'Will I really bear a child, old as I am?' Is anything too marvelous for the Lord to do?" (Genesis 18:13-14) (The event includes several verses, so I read Genesis 18:10-14).

2. I sit for a moment and think about what's happening in the scene. I might even place myself in it if this helps me to understand it better. For me the scene is about doubt, hopelessness, impossibility, difficulty believing God.

3. I just start talking to Jesus. There is no formula

here! This is whatever you feel like talking about. The scene reminds me of doubt, of Jesus hanging on the Cross, hopelessness and failure. I ask Jesus why He sometimes allows things to look utterly hopeless. I sit and listen for His response, which again isn't necessarily audible. I might ask him questions. I often get bold, and ask Him... Is solving a problem in my family too marvelous for the Lord to do? Is solving a problem with my friends too marvelous for the Lord to do? Jesus wants you to be honest with Him. I remember that Jesus is God, and I can't hide my feelings from Him, which leads me to be very open and bold with Him. This leads to a conversation where I experience thoughts coming to me as Jesus' responses. If the conversation gets dry, I start reading from a spiritual book or the Bible. The saints recommend focusing on Jesus' Passion, but you're not limited to this.

4. I start to "hear" Jesus' response. Thoughts come to me. I think of Psalm 77:12 *I will recall the deeds of the LORD; yes, recall your wonders of old.* I remember how Jesus helped me in grade school. I remember times that looked bleak in 7th grade where Jesus helped me. I remember times where help seemed to arrive from nowhere. I "recall the deeds of the Lord." Jesus seems to remind me of these. I see that things may be hopeless, but for Him, there is nothing "too marvelous" to do.

5. The conversation leads to a resolution of some

type which in my case is to trust more and persist in this prayer effort.

I can't emphasize strongly enough – there is no complicated formula here. Find a Biblical passage that moves you, think about it, and start talking. That's it! If you want more structure, look at Pope Francis' or Pope Benedict's format on Lectio Divina online, but you don't have to use this.

How long should you pray? When starting out, you may only be able to go for 5-10 minutes. As hard as it is to believe, over time, you will want to pray longer. Saint Teresa of Avila, a "Doctor of the Church," (regarded as especially authoritative) set a long term goal of 30 minutes day, but you can't start out with that. Saint Teresa is known as the Doctor of Prayer.

My Own Conversational Prayer: What did Jesus and I Talk About?

The teens in my Confirmation class asked me this. As I have emphasized, God desires a very personal relationship with each of us. This goes against common opinion, as many see God as just "floating around out there," watching from a distance. This is the God of Deism, and Deism is a heresy. The exact opposite is true. Why do I bring this up? Jesus and I talked about very personal things, very specific details about my life. In fact, because Jesus is a personal God, I can't tell you exactly what we talked about. This conversation may seem a bit obscure, because it is so personal, so specific to my life.

In high school, I took what may be the best picture of my life, my senior graduation picture. In my conversations with Jesus, I could hear Him (not audibly) bring up this topic. During my prayer, thoughts and ideas came to me that were not my own. Jesus was communicating to me that, even in this aspect of my life, He was directly involved, orchestrating events to my benefit. Why was my graduation picture important? At first, it wasn't entirely clear to me.

In homeroom, I sat behind Brendan, and Brendan and I became good friends. Brendan was a little unusual in that he always wore a nice jacket. Granted, we were in a private school, but as far as I can remember, I wouldn't have found two guys in the school wearing a nice jacket. When picture day arrived, I had completely forgotten. I was up late the night before and hadn't taken a shower that morning. Fortunately, Brendan was in school, and as always, he wore his nice jacket and tie. As fortune would have it, Brendan and I were the same size. After Brendan took his picture, he handed me the jacket and tie. Strangely, they complemented my shirt, and as I said, they fit perfectly. I'm normally a bit camera shy, but the photographer accommodated me, and my picture came out perfectly.

After pictures were published, there was a stir in the

cafeteria. Another friend of mine made a big deal about my picture. Several other people commented about it. It was clear that everything came together for me in my graduation picture. As I conversed with Jesus, He enabled me to connect the dots. I don't take credit for the picture; I had not even taken a shower that morning. Why would my graduation picture be so important? I asked Jesus.

Out of the blue, an answer came to mind. I remembered that I used my graduation picture to apply to a college that was difficult to get into. The college laid a strong emphasis on photos during the application process. I had the sense that my picture made the difference. I knew for certain that this was not my thought; it came to me from Someone else. For personal reasons, I can't explain why this picture was so important. It affected my spiritual life in important ways, preventing me from attending a different college with someone who was a source of sin in my life. This thought was new to me, and I had never considered it before. I had forgotten all about Brendan's jacket, the fact that it was right there when I needed it, the fact that it fit perfectly, and how the photographer did a great job. The conversation left me with a strong feeling of Jesus' Providence and His personal involvement in my life. This enabled me to trust in Jesus; it encouraged me to have regular conversation with Him.

PERSIST

One thing you will need is persistence. Prayer will inevitably become dry at times, and distractions will inevitably occur (which are unavoidable to some extent). At these times, you will need to persist.

If I omitted the following from the Catechism of the Catholic Church, I would be remiss. I am going to give you all the straight truth; I'm not going to sugar-coat it. You don't want me to sugar-coat it. This statement is from Saint Alphonsus Liguori, Doctor of the Church. Prayer is essential. Relationships, by nature, require constant communication to endure. Without this communication, relationships fade. Jesus wants to give us graces, which we need, but He requires that we persistently ask for them.

CCC 2744: Those who pray are certainly saved; those who do not pray are certainly damned.

My goal is not to scare anyone, but I'm not here to sugar-coat either. Jesus Himself had to pray, and the Bible talks about how He would spend long periods in prayer. Prayer will give you the strength to avoid sin and follow Jesus' commandments and teachings. Persistent prayer will powerfully lead you towards Heaven. Your regular conversation with Jesus will give you quite a bit of peace on Earth, and lead you towards happiness forever in Heaven.

The HUGE Power of Prayer

Remember, God misses nothing. He sees all of your difficulties and understands all of your fears.

Does the one who shaped the ear not hear? The one who formed the eye not see? (Psalm 94:9)

I want to underscore the huge, huge, huge power of prayer. We have forgotten the many, many places in the Bible where God promises to be receptive and hear us, when it is for our good. There are countless places in the Bible where God encourages us to pray to Him. He would never encourage us if He did not intend to help us and/ or answer us. Keep in mind, however, that God wants to do much more than provide a one-time answer for something you need; He is looking for something deeper, spending time with you and engaging in a relationship that is unlike any other. He wants you to become His child. Some of my favorite verses are below. In 2 Kings, God, a Personal God, speaks directly to King Hezekiah and says that He has seen his tears.

- *Go back and tell Hezekiah, the leader of my people: Thus says the LORD, the God of David your father: I have heard your prayer; I have seen your tears. Now I am healing you...* (2 Kings 20:5)
- *In my distress I called out: LORD! I cried out to my God. From his temple he heard my voice; my cry to him reached his ears.* (Psalm 18:7)

- *For I know well the plans I have in mind for you—oracle of the LORD—plans for your welfare and not for woe, so as to give you a future of hope. When you call me, and come and pray to me, I will listen to you.* (Jeremiah 29:11-12)
- *Before they call, I will answer; while they are yet speaking, I will hear.* (Isaiah 65:24)
- *Have no anxiety at all, but in everything, by prayer and petition, with thanksgiving, make your requests known to God.* (Philippians 4:6)
- *Trust God at all times, my people! Pour out your hearts to God our refuge!* (Psalm 62:9)

HOW TO PRAY THE ROSARY ... INCLUDING MEDITATIONS ON THE SCIENTIFIC EVIDENCE

Note: I include meditations based on the Shroud, but I leave it to the reader to make their own decision about the Shroud's actual authenticity. The heart of this prayer is meditation, the consideration of the lessons of the mystery and how these apply to our own life. There are countless insights to be drawn from each mystery, and I will cover some of them.

This prayer is very simple. The Rosary consists of twenty mysteries or decades, although typically five decades are prayed at a time. It takes about twenty minutes to pray five decades. Twenty minutes seems like a long time, but after you have prayed the Rosary for awhile, it will seem much shorter.

Each decade, as the name implies, consists of ten Hail Marys, plus one Our Father or eleven prayers in all. This is the bulk of the Rosary, the Our Father and the Hail Mary. As you pray, your mind is concentrating on a particular mystery. First, I cover the prayers you need to know; next, I cover the mysteries. The Our Father and

Hail Mary make up about 95% of the Rosary, so once you have these, you know the lion's share. For the most part, you pray the Our Father and the Hail Mary, and you think about each mystery.

The Prayers that Make up the Rosary

- Our Father
- Hail Mary
- Glory Be
- Apostles' Creed
- Hail Holy Queen
- Fatima Prayer (This prayer was requested by the Blessed Mother in her apparitions at Fatima)

These prayers are often said in a group, so I will present them this way. They can, however, be said privately if you prefer.

Our Father

Leader: Our Father, who art in heaven; hallowed be Thy name; Thy kingdom come; Thy will be done on earth as it is in heaven.

All: Give us this day our daily bread; and forgive us our trespasses as we forgive those who trespass against us, and lead us not into temptation; but deliver us from evil. Amen.

Hail Mary

Leader: Hail Mary, full of grace, the Lord is with thee; blessed art thou among women, and blessed is the fruit of thy womb, Jesus.

All: Holy Mary, Mother of God, pray for us sinners, now and at the hour of our death. Amen.

Glory Be

Leader: Glory be to the Father, and to the Son, and to the Holy Spirit.

All: As it was in the beginning, is now, and ever shall be, world without end. Amen

Apostles' Creed

I believe in God, the Father Almighty, Creator of heaven and earth; and in Jesus Christ, His only Son, our Lord; Who was conceived by the Holy Spirit, born of the Virgin Mary, suffered under Pontius Pilate, was crucified, died, and was buried. He descended into hell; on the third day He arose again from the dead. He ascended into heaven, and sits at the right hand of God, the Father Almighty; from thence He shall come to judge the living and the dead. I believe in the Holy Spirit, the Holy Catholic Church, the communion of Saints, the forgiveness of sins, the resurrection of the body and life everlasting. Amen.

Hail Holy Queen

HAIL, HOLY QUEEN, Mother of Mercy, our life, our sweetness and our hope! To thee do we cry, poor banished children of Eve; to thee do we send up our sighs, mourning and weeping in this vale of tears. Turn then, most gracious advocate, thine eyes of mercy toward us, and after this our exile, show unto us the blessed fruit of thy womb, Jesus. O clement, O loving, O sweet Virgin Mary!

V. Pray for us, O Holy Mother of God.
R. That we may be made worthy of the promises of Christ.

Concluding Prayer

Let us pray. O GOD, Whose only begotten Son, by His life, death, and resurrection, has purchased for us the rewards of eternal life, grant, we beseech Thee, that meditating upon these mysteries of the Most Holy Rosary of the Blessed Virgin Mary, we may imitate what they contain and obtain what they promise, through the same Christ Our Lord. Amen.

Fatima Prayer (prayed at the end of each decade)

All: O my Jesus, forgive us our sins, save us from the fires of hell, lead all souls to Heaven, especially those who have most need of your mercy.

Order of Rosary Prayers

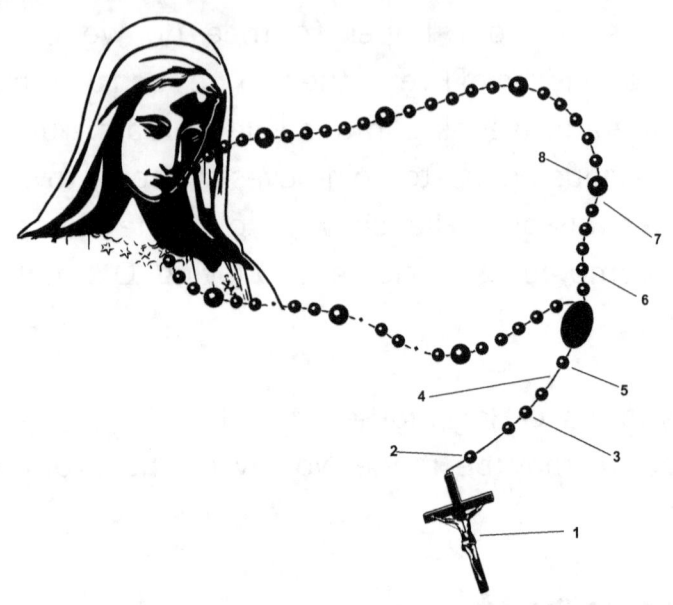

You pray the Apostles Creed on the crucifix (1). You next pray the Our Father and three Hail Marys (2 and 3 above). You pray the Glory Be (4 above). You then begin the First Mystery with an Our Father (5). Each mystery consists of one Our Father and ten Hail Marys followed by a single Fatima Prayer. As you pray, you "meditate" or consider the scene of the particular mystery and the lessons that can be learned from it.

First Joyful Mystery: the Annunciation

Scriptural Excerpt: *Then the angel said to her, "Do not be afraid, Mary, for you have found favor with God. Behold, you will conceive in your womb and bear a son, and you shall name him Jesus. He will be great and will be called Son of the*

Most High, and the Lord God will give him the throne of David his father, and he will rule over the house of Jacob forever, and of his kingdom there will be no end. (Luke 1:30-33)

Meditation: In Luke 1:26, the angel Gabriel (whose name means "God is my Strength") approaches Mary. He tells her that she is to become the Mother of God. He tells her that her Son, Jesus, will be the "Son of David," the long-awaited Messiah promised to the Jewish people ... the Savior of the world.

God actually becomes a Man; the Son of God becomes incarnate in the womb of Mary. Mary takes Jesus into herself, and she gives Him to the entire world; Mary carries the Son of God to the world.

We also take in Jesus every time we receive Him in Holy Communion. Jesus depends upon us to carry Him to the world. Do we believe that the Eucharist is truly Jesus Christ ... Body, Blood, Soul and Divinity? Do we avail ourselves of the Eucharist? Without the strength of Jesus in the Eucharist, we will weaken; we need the strength and support of Jesus in the Eucharist to bring Him to the hopeless, to those around us. Gabriel's name, "God is my Strength," applies to us, and we will find that the Eucharistic Christ is our strength. How do we know Jesus is really in the Eucharist? Jesus has provided Eucharistic Miracles to make this clear. When the Host turns into living heart tissue, verified by scientific analysis, it is clear that the Son of God is in our midst. I cover Eucharistic

Miracles above. Jesus' greatest desire is to unite Himself with us through Holy Communion, and He awaits our visit living as a Prisoner in the tabernacle. The Eucharist gives new meaning to the name Emmanuel, God Who is with us, as He is truly present with us, physically.

Second Joyful Mystery: the Visitation

Scriptural Excerpt: *When Elizabeth heard Mary's greeting, the infant leaped in her womb, and Elizabeth, filled with the holy Spirit, cried out in a loud voice and said, "Most blessed are you among women, and blessed is the fruit of your womb. And how does this happen to me, that the mother of my Lord should come to me? For at the moment the sound of your greeting reached my ears, the infant in my womb leaped for joy. Blessed are you who believed that what was spoken to you by the Lord would be fulfilled."* (Luke 1:41-45)

Meditation: In the second mystery, Mary visits her cousin Elizabeth, who is pregnant with John the Baptist. The story is presented in Luke 1:39. As the angel Gabriel revealed to Mary at the Annunciation, Elizabeth has conceived in her old age. Being elderly, Elizabeth requires a lot of help with this new pregnancy. Elizabeth, who was barren, has now conceived, because *nothing will be impossible for God.* (Luke 1:37)

Imagine how Mary and Elizabeth enjoyed one another's company, how they shared their happiness over the miracles God was performing in their lives. Each of them needed someone who could understand what they were going through, and God provided this. I can only guess that miraculous births such as these would require a lot of personal support.

God also grants Mary evidence to support the validity of her visit by the angel Gabriel. (Gabriel told Mary Elizabeth was pregnant.) God is willing to provide evidence to help support our faith. He asks for faith, but He is also willing to provide some evidence. Many of us are looking for evidence that Christianity and the Catholic Church are real. I provide such evidence when discussing the "Big Three" above, Eucharistic Miracles, Juan Diego's tilma, and the Shroud of Turin.

Third Joyful Mystery: the Nativity

Scriptural Excerpt: *And Joseph too went up from Galilee from the town of Nazareth to Judea, to the city of David that is called Bethlehem, because he was of the house and family of David, to be enrolled with Mary, his betrothed, who was with child. While they were there, the time came for her to have her child, and she gave birth to her firstborn son. She wrapped him in swaddling clothes and laid him in a manger, because there was no room for them in the inn.* (Luke 2:4-7)

Meditation: No one gives Jesus a place to lay His head. He is forced to take the worst place available, the place no one wants. Strangely, I myself have been stranded on two Christmas nights. In both cases, I had car trouble, and I struggled to find a place to stay; I struggled to find shelter from the cold. It was a miserable experience.

I ask myself, will I allow Jesus to stay with me? When He knocks on the door of my heart (perhaps when the poor need alms), do I tell Him to move on? You never know how Jesus will show up; He is truly the Master of Disguise. He might show up as an unborn baby, as He did on the very first Christmas. He might show up as a friend that needs your help. Do I give Jesus the place of honor in my heart, or do I relegate Him to the "barn"? Is He surrounded by passions and sins in my heart, sins I have accepted (the "animals"), or have I cleaned my heart of these, giving Jesus the best room in my house? Do I adore Jesus in Eucharistic Adoration? Am I familiar with recent Eucharistic miracles where the Host has changed into living heart tissue?[99]

Fourth Joyful Mystery: the Presentation

Scriptural Excerpt: *When the days were completed for their purification according to the law of Moses, they took him up to Jerusalem to present him to the Lord, just as it is written in the law of the Lord, "Every male that opens the womb shall be consecrated to the Lord," and to offer the sacrifice of "a pair of turtledoves or two young pigeons," in accordance with the dictate in the law of the Lord.* (Luke 2:22-24)

---

[99] Tesoriero, *Reason to Believe: A Personal Story*, 90-97; Real Presence Eucharistic Education and Adoration Association, The Eucharistic Miracles of the World, 2-7.

Meditation: Mary and Joseph, in obedience to God's commandments, present Jesus in the Temple. Here, I am reminded that loving God includes honoring His commandments. I think of John 14:21:

Whoever has my commandments and observes them is the one who loves me. And whoever loves me will be loved by my Father, and I will love him and reveal myself to him.

I remember Jesus' words to the rich young man in Matthew 19:17:

...If you wish to enter into life, keep the commandments.

I forget that my life is about God's glory (glorifying God in the Temple) rather than about my glory. Sacrifices were made in the Temple, and one important sacrifice is obeying God's commandments. As Mary and Joseph obey God's commandments in the Temple, God in fact reveals Himself to them, through the visits of Simeon and Anna. Simeon takes the baby Jesus, holds Him in his arms, and calls Him *a light for revelation to the Gentiles and glory for your people Israel.* (Luke 2:32) Anna *spoke about the child to all who were awaiting the redemption of Jerusalem.* (Luke 2:38)

Fifth Joyful Mystery: The "Teenage Mystery," the Finding in the Temple

Scriptural Excerpt: *When his parents saw him, they were astonished, and his mother said to him, "Son, why have you done this to us? Your father and I have been looking for you with great anxiety." And he said to them, "Why were you looking for me? Did you not know that I must be in my Father's house?" But they did not understand what he said to them. He went down with them and came to Nazareth, and was obedient to them; and his mother kept all these things in her heart.* (Luke 2:48-51)

Meditation: After celebrating the Passover in Jerusalem, Jesus remains behind as Mary and Joseph head home. Later, noticing His absence, they search for Him with great anxiety. They find Him in the Temple, talking to the teachers of the Law and asking them questions. When Mary and Joseph upbraid Him, He provides a very mysterious response. In the Douay-Rheims Bible translation, to paraphrase, Jesus asks Mary and Joseph if they know that He must be busy doing His father's "business." (Luke 2:49)

I have named this the "Teenage Mystery" because I believe it is very relevant to teenagers. Jesus is twelve years old, about to turn thirteen and become a man in the Jewish tradition. In the presence of His foster father, Joseph, Jesus says that He must be about His father's business. He is speaking of His Heavenly Father. Jesus chooses His Heavenly Father's will as His top priority (which, undoubtedly, Mary and Joseph taught Him to do). As a young man, Jesus is taking personal responsibility for His life, and the first order of business is to discover and follow the Heavenly Father's will. I believe that the twelve-year-old Jesus is teaching us a very important truth. Part of becoming a man or a woman is realizing the primacy of God's will in our life.

First Sorrowful Mystery: Agony in the Garden

Scriptural Excerpt: *Then they came to a place named Gethsemane, and he said to his disciples, "Sit here while I pray." He took with him Peter, James, and John, and began to be troubled and distressed. Then he said to them, "My soul is sorrowful even to death. Remain here and keep watch." He advanced a little and fell to the ground and prayed that if it were possible the hour might pass by him; he said, "Abba, Father, all things are possible to you. Take this cup away from me, but not what I will but what you will."* (Mark 14: 32-36)

Meditation: Jesus' soul is sorrowful even unto death. He feels overwhelmed by everything that is about to occur. His bloodthirsty enemies are circling all around Him; Judas, His intimate friend, is about to betray Him. He will soon endure horrors, including torture and death. What does He do in the midst of His terror? He immediately prays to His Heavenly Father. He speaks, in very personal and familiar terms, calling Him *"Abba,"* or Daddy. In His darkest hour, He turns to prayer, calling His

Heavenly Father Daddy.

He feels like He can't go on. He wants to avoid all of this. How does He overcome? PRAYER. Because of His Agony, He prays the longer. He teaches us that persevering prayer allows us to face all things. For us, this includes praying the Rosary, the weapon that wins all battles!

Second Sorrowful Mystery: Scourging at the Pillar[100]

Scriptural Excerpt: *But he was pierced for our sins, crushed for our iniquity. He bore the punishment that makes us whole, by his wounds we were healed.* (Isaiah 53:5) *So Pilate, wishing to satisfy the crowd, released Barabbas to them and, after he had Jesus scourged, handed him over to be crucified.* (Mark 15:15)

Meditation: The Shroud of Turin provides a possible picture of the scourging received by Jesus. Jackson reports 372 individual wounds, 159 on the front and 213 on the back of the body. According to the forensic evidence, the beating was extremely severe. The Shroud shows wounds beginning at the shoulders, going down the buttocks and continuing down the back of the legs. The wounds received on the buttocks indicate that the Man of the Shroud was naked during the scourging. The Shroud shows scourge

---

[100] Jackson and the Turin Shroud Center of Colorado, *The Shroud of Turin: A Critical Summary of Observations, Data and Hypotheses*, 47-48.

wounds in the shape of dumbbells, suggesting that a Roman flagrum, or scourging device, produced them. The flagrum contained three cords, each with a set of two dumbbells, designed to tear the victim's flesh. The severity of Jesus' scourging could have caused one of His lungs to collapse. In any event, breathing after the scourging would have been extremely painful for Him.

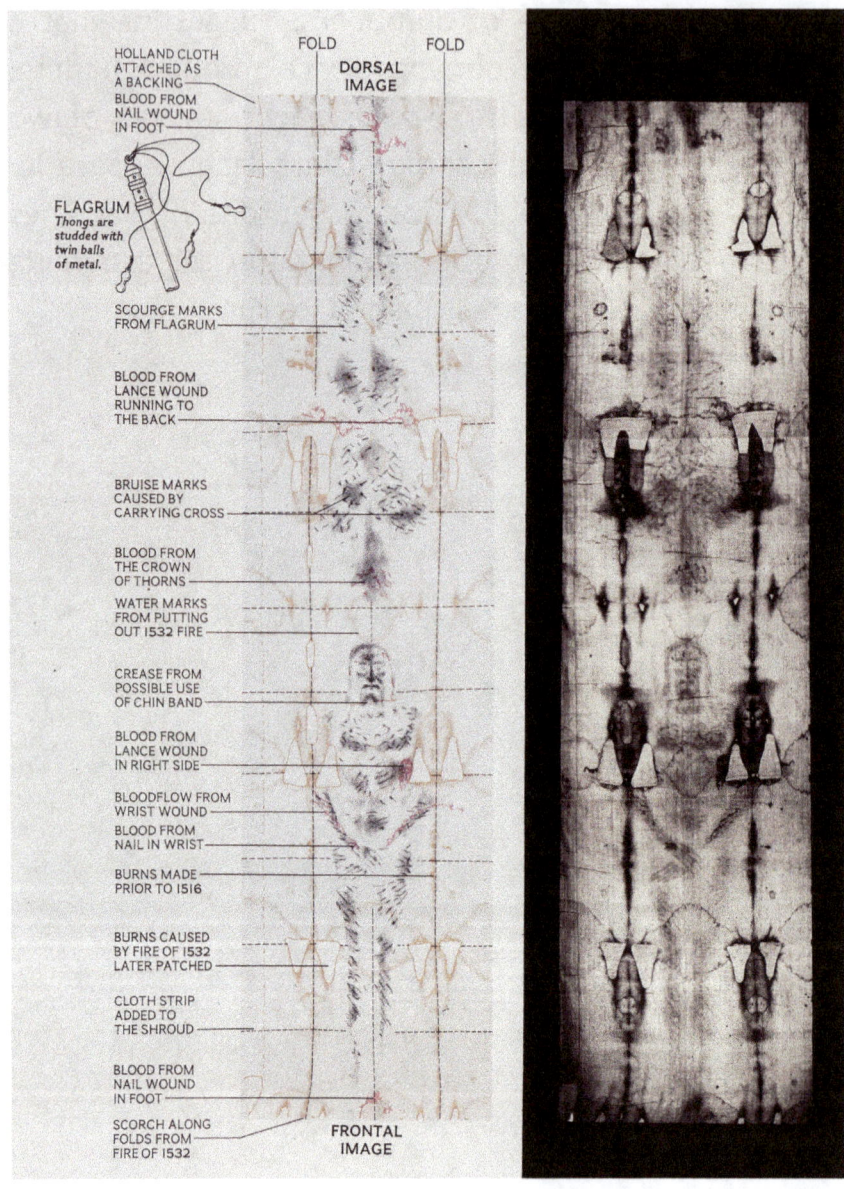

FOLD — DORSAL IMAGE — FOLD

HOLLAND CLOTH ATTACHED AS A BACKING

BLOOD FROM NAIL WOUND IN FOOT

FLAGRUM
Thongs are studded with twin balls of metal.

SCOURGE MARKS FROM FLAGRUM

BLOOD FROM LANCE WOUND RUNNING TO THE BACK

BRUISE MARKS CAUSED BY CARRYING CROSS

BLOOD FROM THE CROWN OF THORNS

WATER MARKS FROM PUTTING OUT 1532 FIRE

CREASE FROM POSSIBLE USE OF CHIN BAND

BLOOD FROM LANCE WOUND IN RIGHT SIDE

BLOODFLOW FROM WRIST WOUND

BLOOD FROM NAIL IN WRIST

BURNS MADE PRIOR TO 1516

BURNS CAUSED BY FIRE OF 1532 LATER PATCHED

CLOTH STRIP ADDED TO THE SHROUD

BLOOD FROM NAIL WOUND IN FOOT

SCORCH ALONG FOLDS FROM FIRE OF 1532

FRONTAL IMAGE

Third Sorrowful Mystery: Crowning with Thorns[101]

Scriptural Excerpt: *Then they spat in his face and struck him, while some slapped him, saying, "Prophesy for us, Messiah: who is it that struck you?"* (Matthew 26:67-68)

Then the soldiers of the governor took Jesus inside the praetorium and gathered the whole cohort around him. They stripped off his clothes and threw a scarlet military cloak about him. Weaving a crown out of thorns, they placed it on his head, and a reed in his right hand. And kneeling before him, they mocked him, saying, "Hail, King of the Jews!" They spat upon him and took the reed and kept striking him on the head. (Matthew 27:27-30)

Meditation: Once again, the Shroud reveals much about Jesus' potential suffering. The Shroud reveals a cap of thorns, rather than a crown, and the cap covered the entire skull. This would have been much more painful than a crown wrapped around the sides of the head. The Shroud reveals more than 30 head wounds. It is difficult to imagine the pain of thorns being pounded into your head. It is equally difficult to imagine the public shame Jesus experienced as He sat humiliated before the people, heralded as a fake, an imposter, with blood and spit running down His face ... the price of our sins of pride

---

[101] Jackson and the Turin Shroud Center of Colorado, *The Shroud of Turin: A Critical Summary of Observations, Data and Hypotheses*, 48-50; Antonacci, *The Resurrection of the Shroud*, 17.

and doubt. Our thoughts of pride have pierced Jesus' head with thorns. Blood from head wounds is directly visible on the Shroud.

The Shroud reveals a swollen nose, and cartilage appears to have separated from the bone. Microscopic analysis shows scratches and dirt on the man's nose. The cheeks and areas above and below the eyes appear swollen, as if someone had beaten the man's face with their fist or another hard object.

Fourth Sorrowful Mystery: Carrying of the Cross[102]

Scriptural Excerpt: *And when they had mocked him, they stripped him of the cloak, dressed him in his own clothes, and led him off to crucify him. As they were going out, they met a Cyrenian named Simon; this man they pressed into service to carry his cross.* (Matthew 27:31-33)

Meditation: The Shroud shows two broad areas of injury across the man's shoulders, suggesting that a heavy wooden beam scraped away his skin. A heavy wooden beam would have exacerbated the suffering, reopening the wounds from the scourging. The Shroud suggests that the man fell under the weight of the beam, and he may have been struck by it falling on top of him. White

---

[102] Jackson and the Turin Shroud Center of Colorado, *The Shroud of Turin: A Critical Summary of Observations, Data and Hypotheses*, 49-50; Antonacci, *The Resurrection of the Shroud*, 20.

light and ultraviolet fluorescent lighting have revealed abrasions and lesions on the front of the man's knees, providing further evidence that he fell as he carried the cross. Microscopic study of the Shroud has found dirt particles on the knees and nose, suggesting that the man fell flat on His face. The crossbeam, or patibulum, weighing as much as 100 pounds, was typically placed behind the head and outstretched arms, secured to the arms with rope. Thus, Jesus' hands were not free, and He couldn't break a fall; He would fall flat on His face.

A severe scourging would have weakened Jesus, making Him prone to falling. Our relapses into sin are often associated with Jesus' repeated falls.

Fifth Sorrowful Mystery: The Crucifixion[103]

Scriptural Excerpt: *When they came to the place called the Skull, they crucified him and the criminals there, one on his right, the other on his left. [Then Jesus said, "Father, forgive them, they know not what they do."] They divided his garments by casting lots. The people stood by and watched; the rulers, meanwhile, sneered at him and said, "He saved others, let him save himself if he is the chosen one, the Messiah of God." Even the soldiers jeered at him. As they approached to offer him wine they called out, "If you are King of the Jews, save yourself." Above him there was an inscription that read,*

---

[103] Jackson and the Turin Shroud Center of Colorado, *The Shroud of Turin: A Critical Summary of Observations, Data and Hypotheses*, 50; Antonacci, *The Resurrection of the Shroud*, 31.

"This is the King of the Jews." (Luke 23:33-38)

Meditation: The Shroud reveals something very interesting about the hand wounds. Although sacred art often depicts nails in the palms of the hands, the Shroud shows nails piercing the wrists. The Shroud shows a nail piercing the back of the left wrist. Forensic scientists have shown that nails in the palms of the hands could not support the weight of a crucified man. Thus, Jesus was likely crucified with nails piercing His wrists. (The word "hand" can be interpreted to include the wrist.) The nail would likely have pulverized or at least detached the median nerve, causing extreme and uninterrupted pain.[104] Of course, Jesus' slightest movement would have amplified this pain.

While hanging from the cross, Jesus' pectoral muscles would contract around His lungs, forcing Him to struggle repeatedly to raise Himself up just to breathe. Jesus would suffer extreme pain as He continued this upward pushing movement, with pain shooting through His wrists every time He moved; He would also experience agonizing pain from pushing upon His impaled feet. Those who have written about this type of execution have described it as a hideous and horrid form of torture.

---

[104] Gerard Joseph Stanley Sr., *He Was Crucified: Reflections on the Passion of Christ* (St. Louis: Concordia Publishing, 2009), 119.

First Glorious Mystery: The Resurrection

Scriptural Excerpt: *Taking the body, Joseph wrapped it [in] clean linen and laid it in his new tomb that he had hewn in the rock. Then he rolled a huge stone across the entrance to the tomb and departed.* (Matthew 27:59-60)

When Simon Peter arrived after him, he went into the tomb and saw the burial cloths there, and the cloth that had covered his head, not with the burial cloths but rolled up in a separate place. Then the other disciple also went in, the one who had arrived at the tomb first, and he saw and believed. For they did not yet understand the scripture that he had to rise from the dead. (John 20:6-9)

Meditation: How does the Shroud provide evidence of the Resurrection? It does so by displaying an image, formed on linen, which cannot be explained without reference to energy or radiation, energy produced by a dead man's body. Dead bodies don't produce energy, and they certainly don't produce particle radiation, the radiation scientists believe created the image on the Shroud.[105] Many have explained the image in other ways, but a true explanation of the image must account for all of the Shroud's properties. As covered above, this includes a number of characteristics, such as the three-dimensional information embedded into the image, the fact that the image is a photographic negative, and the superficiality of the image, just to name a few. The

---

[105] Niyr, *The Turin Shroud: Physical Evidence of Life After Death?*, 75.

Shroud points to the next life, our next life, a life that will never end.

Second Glorious Mystery: The Ascension

Scriptural Excerpt: *When they had gathered together they asked him, "Lord, are you at this time going to restore the kingdom to Israel?" He answered them, "It is not for you to know the times or seasons that the Father has established by his own authority. But you will receive power when the holy Spirit comes upon you, and you will be my witnesses in Jerusalem, throughout Judea and Samaria, and to the ends of the earth."* (Acts 1:6-8)

Meditation: Jesus is asking us to be His witnesses until the day of His return. One way to do this is to assist in teaching Catechism. Teaching Catechism is a great way to learn about your faith and witness to others. If you choose to do this, suddenly, you will feel much more involved with your faith. For those who don't feel called to teaching, I recommend listening to Father Mike Schmitz's Bible in a Year Podcast. You will learn quite a bit about the Bible, and with Father Mike's commentary, you will gain a better understanding of Jesus' words. I've been listening myself. By praying your Rosary, you will learn about the mysteries of our salvation, and this will assist you greatly in witnessing to the faith. Your witness could make all the difference for those around you. Your witness might be the only exposure to Christ they ever receive.

Third Glorious Mystery: Descent of the Holy Spirit

Scriptural Excerpt: *When the time for Pentecost was fulfilled, they were all in one place together. And suddenly there came from the sky a noise like a strong driving wind, and it filled the entire house in which they were. Then there appeared to them tongues as of fire, which parted and came to rest on each one of them. And they were all filled with the holy Spirit and began to speak in different tongues, as the Spirit enabled them to proclaim. Now there were devout Jews from every nation under heaven staying in Jerusalem. At this sound, they gathered in a large crowd, but they were confused because each one heard them speaking in his own language.* (Acts 2:1-6)

Awe came upon everyone, and many wonders and signs were done through the apostles. (Acts 2:43)

Meditation: The Holy Spirit made the disciples courageous. Formerly fearful ... *when the doors were locked, where the disciples were, for fear of the Jews ...* (John 20:19), the disciples are now emboldened. We know that Peter dies as a martyr, being crucified upside down. We know that Paul is martyred as well. Tradition holds that seven other disciples were martyred. One of the seven gifts of the Holy Spirit is Fortitude, moral courage that helps us to stand up for what is right, even when the whole world is against us.

Fourth Glorious Mystery: The Assumption

Scriptural Excerpt: *And Mary said: "My soul proclaims the greatness of the Lord; my spirit rejoices in God my savior. For he has looked upon his handmaid's lowliness; behold, from now on will all ages call me blessed. The Mighty One has done great things for me, and holy is his name.* (Luke 1:46-49)

Meditation: The Mighty One has indeed done great things for Mary, and He wishes to hear His mother praised through the Rosary. Church Tradition teaches that Mary was taken up into Heaven at the end of her earthly life. The Mighty One continues to do great things for Mary, as the Rosary stories attest. Mary is so happy to enter the celestial gates of Paradise that she works tirelessly to bring her children there. She powerfully intercedes with Her Son through the prayer of the Rosary.

Fifth Glorious Mystery: The Coronation of Mary as Queen of Heaven and Earth

Scriptural Excerpt: *A great sign appeared in the sky, a woman clothed with the sun, with the moon under her feet, and on her head a crown of twelve stars.* (Revelation 12:1)

Meditation: Mary has given birth to the King of Kings. This makes her a Queen, and the greatest of Queens. Never, ever ... ever underestimate the powerful influence this Queen wields over the Heart of her Son.

Mary is only a creature like us, but her Son has raised her to the dignity of the Mother of God. Now that she reigns as Queen in Heaven, she intercedes with her Son to obtain all sorts of blessings for her children. In the 5th Promise (from the 15 Promises of the Rosary), Mary says: *The soul which recommends itself to me by the recitation of the Rosary shall not perish.* That's quite a promise, and you can be sure that when she makes such a promise, her Son is right behind her.

The reference to the moon under Mary's feet is brought to life in the miraculous image of Our Lady of Guadalupe on Juan Diego's tilma. Here, Mary is pictured with the moon under her feet, and she wears a mantle of blue-green hue, the color worn by Aztec royalty, indicating that she is a Queen. Her hands are joined in prayer and her head is bowed in reverence, indicating that she cannot be God. She is definitely not God, but she has great influence over His Heart. I present Juan Diego's tilma as one of my three examples of scientifically analyzed evidence for the faith.

Picture shows an artistic representation of miraculous image of Our Lady of Guadalupe. Image by Marcaroni from Pixabay. https://pixabay.com/illustrations/our-lady-of-guada-lupe-4542832/

First Luminous Mystery: The Baptism of Jesus

Scriptural Excerpt: *In those days John the Baptist appeared, preaching in the desert of Judea [and] saying, "Repent, for the kingdom of heaven is at hand!" It was of him that the prophet Isaiah had spoken when he said: "A voice of one crying out in the desert, 'Prepare the way of the Lord, make straight his paths.'" John wore clothing made of camel's hair and had a leather belt around his waist. His food was locusts and wild honey. At that time Jerusalem, all Judea, and the whole region around the Jordan were going out to him and were being baptized by him in the Jordan River as they acknowledged their sins.* (Matthew 3:1-6)

After Jesus was baptized, he came up from the water and behold, the heavens were opened [for him], and he saw the Spirit of God descending like a dove [and] coming upon him. And a voice came from the heavens, saying, "This is my beloved Son, with whom I am well pleased." (Matthew 3:16-17)

Meditation: At the end of our lives, we all want to hear those words from God the Father ... *this is my beloved son ... this is my beloved daughter, with whom I am well pleased*. Sin, however, makes our paths crooked, and it seriously interferes with and can destroy our relationship with God. We are called to *prepare the way of the Lord ... to make straight His paths*. How do we do this? We first have to remove sin from our lives. A great help in doing this is by examining our conscience regularly and receiving Confession, monthly if possible.

Second Luminous Mystery: The Wedding Feast at Cana

Scriptural Excerpt: *On the third day there was a wedding in Cana in Galilee, and the mother of Jesus was there. Jesus and his disciples were also invited to the wedding. When the wine ran short, the mother of Jesus said to him, "They have no wine." [And] Jesus said to her, "Woman, how does your concern affect me? My hour has not yet come." His mother said to the servers, "Do whatever he tells you."* (John 2:1-5)

And when the headwaiter tasted the water that had become wine, without knowing where it came from (although the servers who had drawn the water knew), the headwaiter called the bridegroom and said to him, "Everyone serves good wine first, and then when people have drunk freely, an inferior one; but you have kept the good wine until now." (John 2:9-10)

Meditation: There is a lot happening here. Mary, unasked, seeks to obtain wine for the couple, who have run out. Mary knows that her Son is all powerful, and she knows that He can solve the problem. At Mary's bidding, Jesus performs His first public miracle! Mary's power over the Heart of her Son is on clear display. Notice also how she asks Jesus. She doesn't tell Him what to do, but rather trusts that He will do what is best. He tests her faith at first with a reply that seems somewhat strange, but He eventually gives in. Jesus provides great wine, and lots of it!

Notice how gracious Mary is, seeking to help the unhappy couple even before anyone asks her to do so! She does even more when specifically asked! If you approach her as a trusting child seeking her help, she will intercede for you and work wonders. A great way to approach her, a way she herself has strongly recommended, is to pray the Rosary.

Third Luminous Mystery: The Proclamation of the Kingdom

Scriptural Excerpt: *After John had been arrested, Jesus came to Galilee proclaiming the gospel of God: "This is the time of fulfillment. The kingdom of God is at hand. Repent, and believe in the gospel."* (Mark 1:14-15)

The seventy[-two] returned rejoicing, and said, "Lord, even the demons are subject to us because of your name."

Jesus said, "I have observed Satan fall like lightning from the sky. Behold, I have given you the power 'to tread upon serpents' and scorpions and upon the full force of the enemy and nothing will harm you. Nevertheless, do not rejoice because the spirits are subject to you, but rejoice because your names are written in heaven." (Luke 10:17-20)

Meditation: "... for I shall not pass this way again." This is an old saying, and I can't help but think of it here. *This is the time of fulfillment ... repent and believe.* This moment in your life is unique and unrepeatable. The people in your life, the classes you're taking, the difficulties you're experiencing ... none of this will ever happen again; it will never happen just the way that it is happening today. Eternity is fast approaching, and eternal life is being offered to us in a unique way ... today. Will it be offered to us 5 years from now? There's no guarantee. Jesus says that now is the time to repent.

The seventy-two returned from preaching the Kingdom of God. Jesus tried to focus them. The most important thing to rejoice about is getting into Heaven.

Fourth Luminous Mystery: The Transfiguration

Scriptural Excerpt: *Jesus took Peter, James, and John his brother, and led them up a high mountain by themselves. And he was transfigured before them; his face shone like the sun and his clothes became white as light.* (Matthew 17:1-2)

While he was still speaking, behold, a bright cloud cast a shadow over them, then from the cloud came a voice that said, "This is my beloved Son, with whom I am well pleased; listen to him." When the disciples heard this, they fell prostrate and were very much afraid. But Jesus came and touched them, saying, "Rise, and do not be afraid." (Matthew 17:5-7)

Meditation: I have often pondered that we have no idea how beautiful God is. A beautiful sunset, picturesque beach, and the endless Milky Way ... perhaps these are only the beginning of God's beauty. We're dealing with Someone whose glory we have never seen, whose abilities we have barely observed. For me, this raises the question. What am I not seeing? Who am I not experiencing? We have no idea what we are missing if we don't develop a personal relationship with Him. How can we know what we've never experienced? Are we missing the Pearl of Great Price? Peter, James and John receive a special preview of Jesus' glory, and it is overwhelming. Jesus, knowing that they would soon see Him hanging on the cross in apparent failure, allows them to see His glory beforehand. God the Father tells us to listen to His beloved Son. To see Him and know Him as He is, we need to follow His words.

Fifth Luminous Mystery: The Institution of the Eucharist

Scriptural Excerpt: *While they were eating, Jesus took bread, said the blessing, broke it, and giving it to his disciples said, "Take and eat; this is my body." Then he took a cup, gave thanks, and gave it to them, saying, "Drink from it, all of you, for this is my blood of the covenant, which will be shed on behalf of many for the forgiveness of sins."* (Matthew 26:26-28)

I am the living bread that came down from heaven; whoever eats this bread will live forever; and the bread that I will give is my flesh for the life of the world. (John 6:51)

Meditation: This is the center of our faith. The Catechism of the Catholic Church (1324) teaches that the Eucharist is the source and summit of the Christian life. How many religions have a God that becomes a human being, who becomes one of us? How many religions have a God that offers up His life for His creatures? Finally, how many religions have a God who goes further, becoming physically present in the tabernacle 24 hours a day? You won't find this anywhere else. You can visit Him, speak with Him and seek His help, one-on-one; even the people in ancient Israel didn't have it this good. They had to track Jesus down and then fight the crowds to get to Him.

How do I know Jesus is really present in the Eucharist? Eucharistic Miracles, still happening in the twenty-first century, provide scientifically analyzed evidence of this.[106] The Host changes into living heart tissue, which of course is impossible. Well-known scientists, like Dr. Frederic Zugiba (of Columbia University), have performed tests, finding that the Host has become real flesh and blood, containing human DNA and white blood cells.

Jesus is reaching out to you with scientifically analyzed miracles, hoping that you will come to Him in the Eucharist.

---

[106] Tesoriero, Reason to Believe: *A Personal Story*, 90-97; Real Presence Eucharistic Education and Adoration Association, *The Eucharistic Miracles of the World*, 2-7.

BIBLIOGRAPHY

"1st Friday & 1st Saturday Devotions." America Needs Fatima. Accessed June 26, 2022. https://americaneedsfatima.org/blog/1st-friday-1st-saturday-devotions.

Allen, Diane. *Pray, Hope, and Don't Worry: True Stories of Padre Pio Book I*. Padre Pio Press, 2012.

Angel, Jackie Francois. *"How God Answered My Prayer."* Ascension Presents. September 24, 2019. Video. Accessed November 14, 2021. https://youtu.be/AlK_bJqEEU0.

Antonacci, Mark. *The Resurrection of the Shroud*. New York: M. Evans and Company, 2000.

"A Short Biography." Padre Pio Devotions. Accessed August 8, 2021. https://padrepiodevotions.org/a-short-biography/.

Bamonte, Fr. Francesco. *The Virgin Mary and the Devil in Exorcisms*. 2nd English ed. Libertyville, IL: Pope Leo XIII Institute Press, 2014.

Barron, Robert, Bishop, *"Go on a Hero's Journey - Bishop Barron's Sunday Sermon."* August 6, 2022. video, Accessed August 7, 2022. https://youtu.be/V5II3xYWE1w.

"Battle of Lepanto." Wikipedia. Last modified March 3, 2021. Accessed March 28, 2021. https://en.wikipedia.org/wiki/Battle_of_Lepanto.

Benkovic, Johnnette S., and Thomas K. Sullivan. *The Rosary: Your Weapon for Spiritual Warfare*. Cincinnati: Franciscan Media, 2017.

"Best 19 Quotes on the Rosary." TFP Student Action. Accessed October 17, 2021. https://tfpstudentaction.org/get-involved/campus-rosary-crusade/quotes-on-the-rosary.

Bulst, Werner. "The Pollen Grains on the Shroud of Turin." *Shroud Spectrum International* 3, no. 10 (March 1984): 25-26.

Calloway, MIC, Donald H. *10 Wonders of the Rosary*. Stockbridge, MA: Marian Press, 2019.

Circelli, Jerry. "Renowned researcher Dr. John Jackson reveals his findings about the Shroud of Turin at SMG talk." *North Texas Catholic*, December 2, 2013. Accessed September 12, 2021. https://northtexascatholic.org/features-article?r=UGZUJI4J8S.

Cruz, Joan Carroll. *Eucharistic Miracles and Eucharistic Phenomena in the Lives of the Saints*. Charlotte: TAN Books, 1991.

Del Guercio, Gelsomino. "Devil admits to exorcist: 'I'm afraid of the Madonna.'" Aleteia. July 2, 2017. Accessed March 15, 2021. https://aleteia.org/2017/07/02/devil-admits-to-exorcist-im-afraid-of-the-madonna/.

"Eucharistic Miracle of Legnica 1." Real Presence Eucharistic Education and Adoration Association. Accessed August 11, 2020. http://therealpresence.org/eucharst/mir/english_pdf/Legnica1.pdf.

"Eucharistic Miracle of Legnica 2." Real Presence Eucharistic Education and Adoration Association. Accessed August 11, 2020. http://therealpresence.org/eucharst/mir/english_pdf/Legnica2.pdf.

Hallenbeck, Chris. *The Miraculous 54 Day Rosary Novena to Our Lady*. Gloversville, NY: Great Point Publishing, 2019.

"'I am your mother': Our Lady of Guadalupe." Society of Saint Pius X. December 11, 2014. Accessed October 24, 2021. https://sspx.org/en/i-am-your-mother-lady-of-guadalupe.

Jackson, John, and the Turin Shroud Center of Colorado. *The Shroud of Turin: A Critical Summary of Observations, Data and Hypotheses*. Colorado Springs: The Turin Shroud Center of Colorado, 2017.

Johnston, Francis. *The Wonder of Guadalupe*. Charlotte: TAN Books, 1981.

Kearse, Kelly. "Blood on the Shroud of Turin: An Immunological Review." Shroud of Turin Website. 2012. https://www.shroud.com/pdfs/kearse.pdf.

Landry, Fr. Roger J. "From Satanist to Saint." CatholiCity. October 31, 2008. Accessed March 20, 2021. https://www.catholicity.com/commentary/landry/00691.html.

Leonard, Cheryl. *The Shroud of Turin: The Scientific Evidence*. 2015.

"Mental Prayer." The Spiritual Life. Accessed July 17, 2022. https://slife.org/mental-prayer/

Mesina, Fra. Gabriel M. "Christ and Mary revealed in Genesis 3:15." *Missio Immaculatae Magazine*, May 24, 2017.

Niyr, Mark. *The Turin Shroud: Physical Evidence of Life After Death?* Morgan Hill, CA: Bookstand Publishing, 2020.

Ogunu, Michael. "The Rosary: A Weapon to Win All Battles." *The Southern Cross*, October 31, 2017. Accessed November 14, 2021. https://www.scross. co.za/2017/10/the-rosary-a-weapon-to-win-all-battles/.

"Padre Pio on the Blessed Virgin Mary and the Rosary." *Infallible Catholic* (blog). May 5, 2012. Accessed November 14, 2021. http://infallible-catholic. blogspot.com/2012/05/padre-pio-on-blessed-virgin-mary-and.html.

Pius IX. *Ineffabilis Deus*. Apostolic Constitution. Papal Encyclicals Online. December 8, 1854. Accessed November 14, 2021. https://www.papalencyclicals. net/pius09/p9ineff.htm.

Real Presence Eucharistic Education and Adoration Association. *The Eucharistic Miracles of the World: Catalogue of the Vatican International Exhibition*. 2nd ed. Eternal Life, 2016.

"*Rosary saves 9-11 survivor*." America Needs Fatima. October 17, 2018. Video. Accessed November 14, 2021. https://youtu.be/Jkc_kpwiWQQ.

Schwortz, Barrie. "*The Shroud and the Jew: Barrie Schwortz at TEDx ViadellaConciliazione*." TEDx Talks. May 1, 2013. Video, 7:00. Accessed November 14, 2021. https://youtu.be/4G4sj8hUVaY.

Socci, Antonio. *The Fourth Secret of Fatima*. Fitzwilliam, NH: Loreto Publications, 2006.

Stagnaro, Angelo. "Blessed Bartolo Longo: The Ex-Satanist On the Path to Sainthood." *The Catholic Herald* (London), Jul. 19, 2011.

Stanley Sr., Gerard Joseph. *He Was Crucified: Reflections on the Passion of Christ*. St. Louis: Concordia Publishing, 2009.

Sullivan, OP, Br. Ezra. "The Rosary: The Devil's Defeat." Catholic Exchange. October 26, 2007. Accessed March 21, 2021. https://catholicexchange.com/the-rosary-the-devils-defeat.

Sungenis, Robert A. "New Discoveries of the Constellations on the Tilma of Our Lady of Guadalupe." *Catholic Apologetics International* (2007).

Tesoriero, Ron. *Reason to Believe: A Personal Story*. Australia: Self-published, 2007.

"The 15 Promises of the Blessed Virgin Mary to Catholics who pray the Rosary everyday." Accessed October 18, 2021. www.rosarypromises.com.

Treece, Patricia. *Meet Padre Pio: Beloved Mystic, Miracle Worker and Spiritual Guide*. Cincinnati: Charis, 2001.

Verschuuren, Gerard. *A Catholic Scientist Champions the Shroud of Turin*. Manchester, NH: Sophia Institute Press, 2021.